MW01520073

Just Say Yes!

Just say Yes!

HOW REAL-LIFE ROMEOS (AND JULIETS) POPPED THE QUESTION

Kathryn Mills, Debbie Appel, and Kristan Ginther

RENAISSANCE BOOKS
Los Angeles

to special moments everywhere and the people who create them

Copyright © 1999 by Kathryn Mills, Debbie Appel, and Kristan Ginther

All rights reserved. Reproduction without permission in writing from the publisher is prohibited, except for brief passages in connection with a review. For permission, write: Renaissance Books, 5858 Wilshire Boulevard, Suite 200, Los Angeles, California 90036.

Library of Congress Cataloging-in-Publication Data
[tk]

10 9 8 7 6 5 4 3 2 1

Design by Lisa-Theresa Lenthall

Published by Renaissance Books
Distributed by St. Martin's Press
Manufactured in the United States of America
First Edition

ACKNOWLEDGMENTS

A huge thank-you goes out to all of the couples around the world who sent us their romantic and unique marriage proposal stories. Without them, this book would not have been possible. We are very grateful to them for letting us share these personal moments in their lives. We truly enjoyed reading every submission, whether it made it into the book or not.

We are grateful to the publications and organizations across the United States who helped us gather stories for this book including: *Inside Edition; Essence, Bridal Guide,* and *American Woman* magazines; *UCLA Alumnews; Times-Picayune* (New Orleans, LA), *La Jolla Light* (La Jolla, CA), *Daily Herald* (Arlington Heights, IL), *Herald-News* (Wolf Point, MT), *Putnam County Courier* (Carmel, NY), *Herald American* (Syracuse, NY), and *Dominion Post* (Morgantown, WV) newspapers; Congregation Beth Israel of San Diego; and Bridal Marketing Group–Southern California (800-544-EXPO).

Our heartfelt thanks is extended to the following members of the staff at Renaissance Media: Brenda Scott Royce, Michael Dougherty, Dave Weiner, Bill Hartley, Arthur Morey, Kimbria Hays, Caroline Berkman, Lisa Lenthall, Paula Leto, James Tran, Jesus Arellano, Tina Wilson, Tabitha Thompson, and everyone else who helped and supported us with this project, including our illustrator, Merle Nacht.

We also wish to thank Bob Mills, Daisy Mae Mills, Bob and Laura Mills, Carol Geis, Pat and Susan Schirtzinger, Matt and Vicky Abely, Ed and Kris Fowler-Geis, Ned and Mary Hines, Trish Hines, Grandpa and Jack Markling, Gene and Barbara Appel, Karen Appel, Brian Appel, Jake Appel, Jean Krintzman, Robin Echt, Amy

Rosenberg, Amy H. Stern, Suzanne and Ben Alliker, Rachel Olitsky, Andrew Bauchman, Marion Riemer, Rob May, Michael Weisberg, Gary Keltz, Lisa Jahn-Clough, Dan Cubias, James and Freda Ginther, Donna Ginther and Rodger Erickson, Kandie, Steve, Jason, Casey, and Skylar Flannery, Daisy Cubias, and the rest of our supportive friends and relatives.

INTRODUCTION

Never underestimate the power of eating lunch. One minute you're munching on your favorite sandwich and the next you're coming up with a great idea for a book. At least, that is how this book happened for us.

One warm summer day, we were enjoying each other's company and sharing stories over lunch when Kathryn started to reminisce about how her husband, Bob, had proposed. It was quite a story —creative, romantic, and deeply moving. Let's rewind to that day when Kathryn told us her story:

> Bob and I had been dating for about a year and a half. We ran a Karaoke business in Columbus, Ohio, and we had a show the day after New Year's. While getting ready for the show, Bob suggested that we dress up more than usual to celebrate the New Year. I didn't think twice about it.

> When we arrived, the place was already crowded. Almost all of our friends and family were there. Everyone was having a great time until a gentleman who'd had too much to drink tripped on one of the speaker stands. The speaker fell over and hit Bob's best friend on the head. His girlfriend had to take him to the hospital to get stitches. Well, that was it for me. I was very upset and just wanted to go home, but everyone kept reassuring me that the night was still young.

> We kept the show running. Usually Bob and I will get a chance to sing now and then, but we were so busy that every time Bob asked me if he could sing I said no. But Bob was not about to be

deterred that night. He got ahold of the microphone and said: "This is dedicated to Kathy." Then he sang "Till There Was You" by the Beatles. I was touched and decided to dance with him while he sang.

Everyone started to crowd around us. Some were standing on chairs and the bar just so they could see us. It seemed that almost everyone had a camera in their hands. Bob's dad was even recording it with a video camera. What was I thinking? Gee, isn't it nice that everyone wants to see Bob and me dance? How sweet. When Bob finished singing he turned to me, got down on one knee, and said, "My life has never been better since you've been in it and I want to spend the rest of my life with you. Will you marry me?"

He then opened a ring box and all I could see was this beautiful sparkling diamond ring. I was floored! I started to cry and said, "Yes!"

And here we thought that proposals just all sort of blended together. Then we had an epiphany. Why not write a book about wedding proposals? Thus began our quest for the most romantic, most creative, most fabulous engagement stories ever assembled.

We think we've accomplished this lofty goal. All of the stories in *Just Say Yes!* touched us on a personal level, whether they made us laugh, cry, or shake our heads in awe.

This book is for everyone who has been proposed to, wants to be proposed to, or is just a romantic at heart. You'll be amazed at the lengths some people went just to get a yes out of their mates. Some rented helicopters, or went up in hot-air balloons, rode roller coasters to amaze and stun their partner.

Bashful? Then you'll empathize with those who fell victim to very public proposals. These people were thrust into the spotlight at

Broadway plays, drag races, basketball games—even on national TV. Some of them were so embarrassed they couldn't answer when the question was asked.

And, because sometimes the most romantic gestures are the simplest ones, you'll find some nice, quiet, romantic proposals that will warm your heart. These stories take place in a variety of places—in the woods, on the beach, in a park, or even in the backyard. They involve flowers, teddy bears, candlelit dinners, and always lots of love.

It is our hope that *Just Say Yes!* will also provide valuable advice and inspiration to anyone thinking about proposing to that special someone. This book is packed full of wonderful ideas. Whether you want your proposal to be a private moment between the two of you or you want to go to extremes and make it a big event, you will find plenty of helpful hints in the pages that follow.

What makes *Just Say Yes!* unique is that each story is told in the voice of the person who experienced the event—either as the proposer or proposee. It's as if we were allowed to eavesdrop on more than one hundred intimate, extraordinary engagement moments.

You've heard of feel-good movies. Well, this is a feel-good book. *Just Say Yes!* will take you away to a land where the moments are always special, and if it brings a smile to your face or a tear to your eye, then we've done our job.

So sit back, relax, and enjoy all of the engagement stories from around the world that found their way into *Just Say Yes!* There is a lot of love in this book, and we're very happy to have the opportunity to share it with you.

—Kathryn Mills, Debbie Appel, and Kristan Ginther

TWO GUYS, A GIRL, AND A SHEEP

$\mathcal{B}$eing a hip and modern couple, my girlfriend, Tonya, and I are always striving to break gender roles. The one societal tradition she felt strongly about not breaking, though, was that of the guy asking the girl to marry him. I, on the other hand, thought it would be more fun if I could trick her into proposing to me.

We are a very social couple, always entertaining and having friends over. So when I suggested we have a Halloween party at our apartment, it didn't seem out of the ordinary to Tonya. Unbeknownst to her, I had instructed a few of our friends to come in specific costumes. Jen dressed as a shepherd girl, Ginnie wore a sheep's costume with the symbol for female hung around her neck, and Will did not dress in any costume. I dressed up in Tonya's clothes.

The party was going well and Tonya didn't suspect a thing. The trap was set. Around 11:00 P.M. I asked everyone to come into the living room to play a game. I explained it was a guessing game that only Tonya could play. I lined up my friends: Will, Ginnie, and Jen, and placed myself at the end of the line.

"Who are we?" I asked.

"Well, you're me," Tonya said quickly. "And that's Will."

The other two were a little tougher. After guessing Little Bo Peep and the lost sheep, she settled on Mary and the little lamb. Seeing the lamb had a female sign, she decided it must be a female lamb, or a ewe.

"So, who are we?" I asked again.

"Me and ewe and Mary and Will," Tonya said slowly.

"How about in order?" I laughed.

"Will . . . ewe . . . Mary . . . me," she said.

"Sure, thanks for asking," I said as I retrieved the diamond ring from its hiding place. Tonya looked at me in disbelief as I slipped the ring on her finger. She couldn't believe she'd been trumped. But now she agrees that an old-fashioned proposal just wouldn't have been right for such a contemporary couple.

—*Jason Delborne, Chicago, IL*

SOMETHING SPECIAL IN THE AIR

*M*y fiancé, Jim, and I both work for American Airlines. I am a flight attendant based in Miami, and Jim is a captain based in Washington, D.C. As you might imagine, when Jim is on the job, he's usually very dignified. But as I learned, he has a wild side as well.

We were both working the same flight—Dallas to Vancouver—when we met. After arriving in Vancouver, the flight crew did some sightseeing together. Jim and I hit it off immediately. After the return flight, we exchanged telephone numbers. Our first telephone conversation lasted two hours. We fell in "like" over the phone that night, and we've been dating ever since.

Jim and I happened to be working the same Dallas-Vancouver flight almost a year from the day we first met. We were lined up on the runway to take off, but apparently something was wrong, so Jim parked the plane on an inactive taxiway. Jim emerged from the cockpit, told me that his microphone was not working properly, and said that he wanted to use the microphone near my seat.

Jim picked up the microphone and proceeded to give all the usual flight information (the weather, altitude, and flight time). Then he said, "Before we take off, I would like to ask Aquanetta, my girlfriend and the number one flight attendant, a question. Aquanetta, will you marry me?" The passengers were so excited, they applauded wildly. I grabbed the microphone from Jim and said, "The answer is *yes!*"

—*Aquanetta Johnson, Fort Lauderdale, FL*

PLAY BALL

*L*aurie and I have a history that most couples could only wish for. I saw her on the first day of eighth grade, and every day for the next few weeks I would walk out of my way just to get a glimpse of her. I was on the flag-football team, and one day when she was watching us play, I caught her smiling at me. After the game, we started talking, and that conversation led to a wonderful relationship that continued all through high school. We grew even closer after graduation and by the end of that year, I started thinking about the "M" word.

Unfortunately, my plans were delayed when Laurie's sister, Cindy, was diagnosed with colon cancer that February. We both loved Cindy very much and were deeply affected by her illness. Cindy was a huge San Diego Padres fan and, with a few phone calls to the team's office, a friend of hers arranged for Cindy to throw out the first pitch at Fan Appreciation Night that April. The Padres were extremely supportive throughout Cindy's battle with cancer. They sent her on a dream trip to New York and later cheered her up with a video wishing her good health. Cindy's fight with cancer, however, ended the following January. As a tribute to her, the Padres set up the Cindy Matters Fund in her memory, which supports research for children with cancer.

When talk of marriage between Laurie and I resumed, I knew I wanted to include Cindy's memory in my proposal. That's when I thought of asking the Padres for help in making our engagement special. I called them up and arranged the "big day." The Padres called Laurie's family and asked them to join the team at a game on August 29, when a big company would be contributing a large sum of money to the Cindy Matters Fund. Of course the family was thrilled and accepted the invitation.

We arrived at the stadium on the night of the big event. Before we could get settled in our seats, a member of the Padres' staff asked Laurie to throw out the first pitch in Cindy's honor. Before she could say no, he pulled her onto the field. That's when I sneaked away to complete my plan.

The officials led me into the dugout where I put on the uniform of the Padres' catcher, Carlos Hernandez, complete with a chest pad and catcher's mask. Disguised, I walked onto the field and squatted behind home plate. I could see how excited Laurie was as she threw the first pitch to "Carlos Hernandez." Following tradition, I caught the ball, stood up, and started to walk toward her to return the ball. As I did, I took off my catcher's mask and caught Laurie completely off guard. She was truly shocked to see me approaching her. When I reached the pitcher's mound, I got down on one knee and said, "I know you've waited a long time for this. I love you and I would feel cherished if you would be my wife." Then I opened up a baseball that had been cut in half and hinged. Inside was the diamond she had always dreamed of wearing. Sixty thousand people watched the big screen as Laurie said, "Yes!" In our hearts, that moment of joy was shared with Cindy, who we know was with us in spirit.

—*Robert Davila, San Diego, CA*

SUNKEN TREASURE

*P*roposals can seem to come literally out of the blue. Mine is a good example.

While vacationing in Cozumel over Thanksgiving, my boyfriend and I decided to go scuba diving. The weather was rainy and only a handful of divers were out with us that afternoon. We were thirty feet down under an airplane wreck, when, through the murky water, I saw something sparkling under one of the wings of the plane. As I got closer I could see that it was a heart-shaped crystal box. I swam over and picked it up. Upon closer inspection, I noticed that it was engraved with the words *you found my heart* and the date, November 25, 1997. I didn't even realize it was that day's date.

After we got back on dry land, I asked the other divers and the people in the dive shop if anyone had lost anything. No one had. My boyfriend suggested that maybe it was a store promotion or something. So I put the box in my bag and forgot about it.

Later that evening, back in our hotel room, I came across the box. I decided to take a closer look. There appeared to be a note inside. It took us awhile to open the box, because it was sealed with silicone. I was getting a bit depressed thinking of this lover's note and how its intended would never read it. Finally, we pried the box open. I unfolded the note and found a beautiful diamond solitaire ring. I turned to my boyfriend and noticed that he was down on bended knee. "Will you marry me?" he asked. "I would be honored to," I answered.

—*Julia Victoria Young, Harvey, LA*

WHO WROTE THE BOOK OF LOVE?

*M*y boyfriend, Chris, and I were good friends for about six months before the *When Harry Met Sally* syndrome kicked in and we crossed that "more than friends" line. Shortly thereafter, we spoke about getting married; we even picked out an engagement ring. I knew a proposal was coming . . . I just didn't know when.

When I went to pick up the ring, the jeweler told me there was a problem getting one of the parts for it. I was upset because the ring wouldn't be ready in time for our one-year anniversary—which I thought would be the perfect night for Chris to formalize his proposal to me.

On the night of our anniversary, Chris handed me a gift that was obviously bigger than a ring and said, "I know it's not quite what you want but I'm hoping this will be a good substitute for now." Inside the box was the most incredible scrapbook I had ever seen. The man had saved *everything* since the day we'd first met—pictures, movie ticket stubs, cards, and notes. Everything!

The final page read: "Will you marry me?" I was so surprised that I slammed the book shut. I turned to Chris and saw the ring in his hand. He had picked it up right on schedule and had asked the jeweler to fake me out. I burst into tears! He said, "Well, yes or no?" I replied, "Yes."

The beauty of this proposal is that we will have it forever. Now and then one of us will say, "Go get the book." We then retrieve the scrapbook and relive that glorious time once again.

—*Kristi Miller, Columbia, MO*

SLAM DUNK!

I had known for a long while that my girlfriend, Ducky, was "the one," but she was awfully skittish about the "M" word. She didn't even want to talk about the future until after we'd passed our six-month anniversary. I figured that I would have to wait until at least our one-year anniversary before proposing. But she aced me.

Around our first anniversary, Ducky and I attended a San Jose Lasers game. During the break between the third and fourth quarters, the house Santa Claus, who had been working the crowd all night to promote a Toys-for-Tots program, walked up the stairs to my row. He asked me to stand.

I was confused about the proceedings until I heard the announcer say: "Jim, your girlfriend wants to know if you will marry her!" It took me a long time to process that he was talking to me, that he was talking about marriage, and that my marriage-phobic girlfriend was the person behind it. I didn't even notice the proposal message on the scoreboard until Ducky pointed it out to me.

I was delighted. The crowd gave me a standing ovation. When Santa presented me with a silver bracelet in lieu of a ring, I held it high in the air so that everyone could see. Finally, I turned to Ducky and said, "Yes."

I don't remember a lot of the rest of the game. My heart was so full.

—Anonymous

A, B, C, D, E, F, G

$\mathcal{M}$y husband is a unique man, and, staying true to form, he came up with a unique way of proposing to me.

One Saturday morning, he told me to stay put so he could fix me a special breakfast in bed. He went downstairs to the kitchen and I heard him banging around, making quite a racket. I had no idea what he could be fixing. I didn't even smell any coffee brewing.

When he returned, he was carrying a tray with orange juice, toast, and a bowl of cereal. He put the tray down in front of me and stood back with a huge, goofy grin on his face. I picked up my spoon and went to take a bite of cereal when I stopped, amazed. The bowl was filled with Alpha Bits cereal, and floating in the milk were letters that had been glued together. The letters spelled out "will you marry me." When I realized what it said, I looked up at him. He was holding an open ring box and again asked me to marry him. I didn't have to spell it out for him: My answer was yes!

—*Tia Roseboro, Gahanna, OH*

MUSIC OF THE NIGHT

*M*y boyfriend, Lance, and I had been dating for almost five years. We met in college and I knew immediately that this was the man I wanted to spend my life with. Although we had talked about getting engaged someday, his proposal came as a complete surprise to me. And let me tell you, it was a show-stopper.

At the time, we were living in different cities. I was teaching fourth grade at a school in Pasadena, California, and Lance was working as a consultant in San Francisco. One day, my principal informed me that I was to attend a two-day teaching conference in San Francisco during the first week in March. The conference, location, and dates worked perfectly into my schedule because it coincided with my five-year anniversary of dating Lance.

Over the next few weeks, I received plane tickets to San Francisco, a conference itinerary, and a letter from the superintendent of my school district thanking me for attending the conference. Lance and I had decided to spend a romantic weekend together after the conference, and had planned a quiet, simple dinner on the night of our anniversary. That day, I flew to San Francisco and found Lance waiting for me at the airport with a big bouquet of lavender and pale pink flowers in hand. Happy to be together, Lance and I drove to his apartment to drop off my suitcases and teaching materials. I was anxious to check into the hotel where I'd be staying for the conference, but Lance assured me that I could take care of that later.

He took me to a beautiful little Italian restaurant for dinner. However, while I was enjoying the ambiance and the company, he was rushing us to order and asking the waiter to be quick with our meals. He seemed very unlike his usual calm, easy-going self. I fig-ured he'd had a long day at work and shrugged it off.

After dinner, we rode a cable car into the theater district. We hopped off and strolled down the street, stopping in front of the theater that was featuring *The Phantom of the Opera*. He then pre-sented me with two tickets to the show! On our first date, five years earlier, Lance had taken me to see *Phantom* in Los Angeles, and I was thrilled and impressed by this romantic replay of our first date. We entered the theater and were ushered to our seats.

At the end of the musical, I once again mentioned to Lance that I wanted to check into my hotel so they wouldn't cancel my reserva-tion. He said my reservation would be fine, and that he had arranged for us to get a backstage tour. I was shocked! The stage manager greeted us as we walked onto the stage, and then we were led through a maze of costume rooms, wig departments, and actors' dressing rooms.

After the exciting tour, we were led back up onstage. Most of the audience had left, but the cast members were milling around the stage in their street clothes. We were introduced to everyone, including the lead actors who played Christine and Raoul. They told us they had been requested to sing a special song from the show. They held hands and began to sing the love song, "That's All I Ask of You." Suddenly they stopped singing, and "Raoul" said, "Now Lance has something he wants to say."

I turned to find the "Phantom" presenting Lance with a small box. Lance got down on one knee, opened the box to reveal a beautiful diamond ring, and asked me if I would honor him by becoming his wife. I cried and I think I said yes. The cast members cried, the stage manager took pictures, and they made us feel even more special than I already felt with this amazing ring on my finger and the incredible man standing next to me who would soon be my husband.

We walked outside and crossed the street to the beautiful hotel where we would be staying for the evening. Lance checked us in at the registration desk, and when we opened the door to our room, I heard a loud yell of "Surprise!" My family and Lance's were waiting for us with lots of hugs, loads of excitement, and plenty of cake and champagne to celebrate.

I later found out that Lance had spent months planning this evening with my family, his family, my principal, the superintendent of my school (the "conference" was just a ploy to get me to San Francisco), and the cast members of *The Phantom of the Opera*. I still cannot believe how much planning he did and how many people he worked with to make our engagement night so special and perfect.

—*Jennifer (Janofsky) Ralls, Los Angeles, CA*

THE MOON, THE STARS, AND FIREFLIES

$\mathcal{B}$y the end of our first date, it was obvious that Byron was the one for me. One of the reasons I was sure he loved me was the way he listened to every word I said. When we talked, we talked a lot.

We didn't just make small talk. We had some really far out discussions—like just how many hairs are there on the human head, what color is silence, why are there hardly any fireflies any more, things of that nature. Talk. Talk. Talk. That was us.

As our relationship progressed, we talked about marriage. We both knew that we wanted to spend the rest of our lives together, but we decided that we would not become officially engaged until we had both experienced "the moment." That absolute moment when you truly know deep down inside that you have found your soulmate.

Byron would swear to me on many occasions over the following months that he had experienced "the moment" and wanted to get engaged. He even went so far as to say that he experienced "the moment" every time he was with me. I almost gave in at that point, but I stayed strong and true to our pact.

One night, Byron picked me up from work and told me that he had a surprise for me. This was nothing new as he was always surprising me. When we got home, he led me straight to the bedroom. He stopped me before I opened the door and said, "Close your eyes."

Then he opened the door, pushed me into the room, and quickly shut the door again. "Okay, open your eyes," he said. I opened them and couldn't see anything. It was pitch black. I kept waiting for something to happen, but nothing did. Just when I was ready to ask him what this was all about, I noticed little tiny, yellow bursts of light all around me.

I started laughing and crying at the same time. Byron had gone into the woods and caught a bedroom full of fireflies. Although it was our deep talks that had brought us closer together, there are moments when actions speak louder than words. This was one of them—this was my "moment." I turned to him and said, "Alright, let's get married."

—*Carrie Bryant, Longview, TX*

FROGNAPPED

$\mathcal{I}$t was an unusually cold, snowy New York Saturday in November. The weather didn't dampen my high spirits, however, because it was my first day off from work after a grueling quarter of master's degree courses. Expecting to relax with my boyfriend, Brian, I hadn't made any plans for the day. I had no idea that by evening's end, I would be Brian's fiancée. Nor could I have guessed that he'd have me jumping through hoops in order to get to the big surprise.

He arrived at my house at approximately 10:00 A.M. and made breakfast for us. As we were finishing up our meal, I received a mysterious phone call. An unfamiliar voice on the other end informed me that he had a little green friend of mine. I knew immediately what he was talking about because I had noticed that my stuffed Kermit the Frog had been missing for a few days. I thought that my roommate's nephew had probably stashed it in a closet somewhere, but the caller confirmed my worst suspicion—Kermie had been frognapped!

The man on the phone began to spell out a Web address letter by letter, dragging out the agony. I quickly ran upstairs to my computer and connected to the Web page. To my horror, a picture appeared of my poor Kermit, bound and gagged, sitting in a dark, dirty place! The message below the picture was clear: If I ever wanted to see Kermit alive again, I must follow all instructions exactly. My first task was to retrieve a note taped on my front porch. In cut-out letters, the note instructed me to attend the noontime showing of *The Little Mermaid*. The frognappers were kind enough to include two tickets to the show, so I took Brian along with me for moral support.

After the movie, several other hidden notes and anonymous phone calls sent me back home, to a park, to the planetarium, and to the café where Brian had first asked me out. In fact, every place we went was a place we visited together early on in our relationship. When I arrived at each location, I was instructed to do some ridiculous things, like reciting a poem to a waitress, but for the sake of the frog I never hesitated.

The last note led us to an exquisite restaurant in downtown Rochester, where we were seated in a semi-private room with a beautiful bouquet on the table. After we finished our desserts, Brian told the waiter that everything was wonderful, but he desired something more. So the waiter brought out our special dessert—a smiling Kermit with a note in his lap. The note explained that something important was taped under Kermit's vest. I lifted up the vest to find an envelope containing a diamond ring. Brian took it and made a beautiful speech ending with "Will you marry me?" Because I was so choked up, I quickly responded with all I could manage to say— "Yep." I felt like leaping across the table and into his arms, but one frog on the table was enough.

—*Rebecca Haak, Rochester, NY*

BUSTED!

I am a public defender for San Diego County. I was in court when I received a call from my supervisor. He told me to report upstairs to Department 4 to cover a case for a colleague. I immediately went upstairs and walked into court. There, I found another one of my supervisors filming the courtroom with a video camera. I asked him what the camera was for and he said that he was doing a training video for the office. The judge took the bench and called the case. When he said "People versus Mark Jones," I didn't think it was unusual because there are tons of men named Mark Jones in the world. But when the bailiffs brought out my then boyfriend with the "jail blues" (waist chains and handcuffs), my heart stopped. I tried to maintain some composure as the judge had the prosecutor and me approach the sidebar.

I asked the judge for permission to speak with "my client," not revealing that I knew Mark. The judge graciously granted my request. I approached Mark who was seated at the defense table. He told me that he had an outstanding traffic warrant. I was about to let him have it when the judge called me back to the sidebar. We discussed the case for a moment and I turned to face Mark once again. He was on one knee, holding a beautiful engagement ring. He proposed to me, and of course, I said yes. The courtroom was now filled with court staff, bailiffs, my supervisors, and fellow attorneys who cheered our engagement. I had to sit down to recover from the shock. Later, we went into the jury deliberation room for cake and punch.

I had to admire my fiancé for thinking up this ingenious proposal, my best friend at work who helped him plan it, and the judge for his ad-libbing skills. You see, Mark was supposed to propose to me after the first sidebar, but the bailiff had gotten a little carried away and handcuffed him to the chair. The judge saw Mark struggling and called me back for the second sidebar. And the training video was part of the scheme to preserve this unique proposal for posterity.

—*Tara L. Moon, Esq., San Diego, CA*

THE RIDE OF MY LIFE

$\mathcal{T}$im and I met on a youth group trip to California when we were in high school. The trip consisted of a day at the beach and another day at Six Flags Magic Mountain amusement park. The biggest roller coaster there is the Viper. It has an eighteen-story drop plus nine loops. You could definitely call this ride intimidating. Tim was scared to go on it, but I am a roller coaster fanatic. He agreed to go with me if I'd sit next to him. This set the tone for our relationship.

After five years together (through the rest of high school and college), we again went on that very same California trip, but this time as youth group leaders. We went to Magic Mountain, and Tim insisted on going on the Viper as the very first ride of the day. I was a little surprised because I thought he would need to warm up on some of the smaller rides. Tim seemed incredibly nervous, a condition which worsened as we neared the front of the line. I was joking with him about being so scared over a roller coaster ride.

We finally boarded the Viper, in the last car. As the car climbed eighteen stories high, Tim turned to me, pulled out a beautiful engagement ring, and said, "Mandy, will you marry me and make the rest of our lives as exciting as this ride is going to be?" I was so shocked that I barely managed to say yes. He handed the ring to me, and I put it on my finger as we dropped eighteen exhilarating stories. The ride did not match the thrill I felt from getting engaged!

—Amanda Ostapuk, Peoria, AZ

POPPING THE QUESTION

During our three-year courtship, my boyfriend, Scott, and I often went on picnics together. So when Scott asked me on a picnic date one Sunday, I had no reason to think it would be a picnic I would never forget.

When we arrived at the park, we spread out our blanket and unpacked our basket. There was a bottle of wine, some sandwiches, and a box of Cracker Jacks for dessert. We soon realized that we had forgotten to pack the bottle opener. Scott lived five minutes from the park, so he volunteered to run home and get it.

Thirty minutes later, there was no sign of Scott. After forty-five minutes, I started to get worried. Then I saw him walking toward me, holding a huge balloon bouquet. There was an enormous white balloon, several small heart-shaped balloons, and a dove balloon that read, "I love you." I asked if he had met a balloon vendor in the park, but he said no. I was touched by his effort, and didn't suspect it was part of a larger plan.

We sat down to eat. I started pouring the wine. Scott stopped me and said, "Angela, I have another surprise for you." He handed me a black velvet ring box. At first, I couldn't do or say anything. I was stunned. I opened the box. To my surprise, instead of a ring, I found a pin with a note that said:

Pop the white one.

It took me a second to realize he meant the white balloon. I popped it with a pin and a piece of paper flew out and spiralled to the ground. On it was written:

Will you marry me? I love you, Scott!

P.S. How's that for popping the question?

P.P.S. Who says there aren't diamonds in the bottom of a Cracker Jacks box?

I burst into tears and excitedly answered yes. I grabbed the Cracker Jacks box and emptied it onto the blanket. Out fell the most beautiful diamond ring. He slipped it on my finger and the rest is history.

—Angela Gerharz, Liverpool, NY

CATCH OF THE DAY

*I*t was June 1947. Times were simpler then. But sometimes the simplest things in life are the sweetest.

One evening, I went to the movies with my steady, Mabry. Afterward, he walked me home and we sat on the porch. He asked me if I could go see the priest the next day, as he was leaving to go fishing on his shrimp boat. I asked, "What should I talk to the priest about?" and he said, "We are getting married, so make all the arrangements." Mabry is a man of few words, but with these few words he captured my heart.

I made the arrangements and we got married June 11, 1947. We're still happily married.

—*Laura Guidry, Galliano, LA*

A PROPOSAL OF EPIC PROPORTIONS

$\mathcal{I}$ had often told Doug, my boyfriend, that someday I dreamed of getting married in Sedona, Arizona. I believed this city to be one of the most gorgeous places on earth and felt that I should be there on the happiest day of my life.

One day, Doug called me at work saying that he had just purchased two round-trip tickets to Sedona. He said that he thought this would be the perfect time to check it out. I asked him if I should wear something white, but he assured me that he wanted to wait a couple of years before tying the knot. My hopes deflated, I bit my lip and vowed to enjoy the weekend anyway.

We flew into Phoenix and then rented a convertible as a special treat for Doug's birthday, which was the next day. From Phoenix, we drove to Sedona, arriving just in time to catch a beautiful sunset. Because Doug was keeping all the details of the trip secret, I did not know where we would be staying. I was shocked when we turned into L'Auberge, an intimate resort tucked in the woods on the outskirts of town. Our cottage was adorable; it even had a view of a winding creek. That evening, we enjoyed a quiet dinner and retired early so we could enjoy the tranquility of our accommodations.

Doug's birthday began with a quiet breakfast by the creek. We spent the afternoon sightseeing and visiting small shops throughout town. At sunset, we went on a "pink jeep" tour of red-rock terrain. We finished the night with a romantic dinner at the resort and fell asleep in a hammock by the creek.

The following day, we visited Slide Rock, a natural water slide, where we waded through freezing cold water. From there, we visited ancient Indian ruins throughout Sedona and spotted some possible sites for our wedding. When we returned to the cottage that afternoon, Doug said that he had one more little surprise for me. He blindfolded me and guided me to the car. After we drove about five minutes, Doug stopped the car and got out. He still insisted that I not peek. Finally, he told me it was okay to take off the blindfold.

We were at an airport. In the distance I noticed a woman flagging us over to a helicopter. We hopped aboard, and as we flew the pilot pointed out the green valleys, breathtaking red-rock terrain, more Indian ruins, and legendary landmarks. At this point all I could say was "Wow."

After a twenty-minute tour, we descended onto a red-rock mesa in the middle of nowhere. As soon as the helicopter landed, Doug pulled me out and led me over to the edge of the mesa. He pointed out all of the amazing sites. It was incredible. I didn't want to return to the landing site, but Doug insisted.

I thought we were going to climb back into the helicopter and leave. However, when we returned to the helicopter, the pilot was nowhere to be found. Doug feigned ignorance, but in the distance I spotted a tiny table for two. It had been set up with white linen, a beautiful meal on fine china, flowers, candles, and champagne. I looked at Doug, who said that he thought that this was the perfect way to end an incredible weekend.

After many hugs and kisses, we sat down to a romantic dinner —just the two of us on a bluff at sunset. As we finished eating, the pilot sauntered into view. He had been hiding behind some rocks to give us some privacy. He informed us that it was time to head back, but first he requested that we pose for a promotional photo. We happily posed for the camera, and at that moment Doug fell (literally) to his knees. He nervously took my hand and said: "You've been so wonderful to me. I truly love you. Will you marry me and be my wife?"

With tears in my eyes and hands trembling, I replied: "Yes, there is nothing in this world that would make me happier." Doug put the ring on my finger as the pilot continued to snap pictures.

When we arrived back at the resort, the concierge greeted us and said that there was champagne waiting for us at the bar. We picked up our glasses of champagne and walked by the creek on our way to the cottage. As we approached the cottage, I looked down to see wildflower petals scattered on the porch. Inside, there was a warm fire burning and there were chocolate-covered strawberries and yet another bottle of chilled champagne. That night we called everyone we knew to share the wonderful news.

We capped off the weekend with a hot air balloon ride at sunrise the next morning. We were married the following year on June 19, Doug's birthday.

—*Sarah Ramsay, Redondo Beach, CA*

UPROAR IN THE OFFICE

On our one-year anniversary, my boyfriend, Anthony, and I chose to celebrate by having a quiet dinner out. However, I was running late because I was stuck at work. He came to my office, a law firm, to wait for me while I finished my project.

During the next ten minutes, he seemed really anxious and fidgety, but I figured he was just tired of waiting. I was glued to my computer, but he kept trying to get me to talk to him by asking me a bunch of questions. "Pumpkin, my nose is runny, could you please pass me some tissue?" I passed him the entire box without turning around. "Pumpkin, isn't this picture of us on your desk *really* nice?" I said, "Yes, I agree" without even looking because I saw it every day. His random questions continued for another few minutes.

Finally, I realized that if I wanted to finish this project before the weekend, I had to get my honey to stop distracting me. I turned around to talk to him and was stunned to see him holding an open box with a beautiful diamond ring inside. With a huge grin on his face, he then asked me to be his wife. Now, I can't sing a note to save my life, but at that moment, I started singing, hollering, and dancing around the room as my way of saying yes! I caused such an uproar that several attorneys (including my boss) came out of their offices to see what had happened.

We were married two years ago and I haven't stopped singing since.

—*Lisa E. Contaste, Stone Mountain, GA*

EGGING HER ON

Sara and I had been friends for about a year before we started dating seriously. We knew after a short while of "going steady" that we were meant for each other, and we began talking about getting married.

We both worked at the local mall and had plenty of time to browse jewelry stores for a ring. After a few short weeks, we narrowed the ring hunt. At the time, I told Sara that the ring she picked was nice, but I couldn't afford it. But the next chance I got, I went back to the store and purchased the ring. It did actually put quite a strain on my pocketbook, but Sara is worth every penny and more.

Now, the tough part: the proposal. I wanted it to be unforgettable, and I waited until Easter (which was about four months away) to do the deed.

Easter arrived, and I decided to send her on an Easter egg hunt with a twist. I purchased five plastic eggs, a dozen red roses, one Easter lily, and an Easter egg basket full of yummy treats.

I left three red roses and a plastic egg with a clue inside it on Sara's desk at work. This first clue sent her to a clothing store in the mall where she found a new Easter dress, three more red roses, and another egg with another clue inside. From the clothing store, Sara next went to a card store. Waiting for her there was a romantic card, three more red roses, and another egg. This clue told her to go home where she found a bottle of her favorite perfume, two more red roses, and another egg. This time, instead of a clue, I left instructions for her to put on her new dress, spray on some perfume, and take all of the roses to her favorite restaurant.

I was waiting at the restaurant with the basket, the final rose, and the Easter lily. Inside the Easter basket, I had placed the final egg. All through dinner, I saw Sara looking at the egg with mounting curiosity. She seemed to suspect that inside the egg was something much more important than another clue.

We finished eating. Nervously, I took the final egg from the basket, got down on one knee, and told her how much she meant to me and that I couldn't imagine my life without her. I then said, "Will you marry me?" To her surprise, I pulled the ring (the very ring that I said I couldn't afford) from the final egg and placed it on her finger. She threw her arms around me and said, "yes, yes, and a thousand times, yes."

—*Christopher Lomelino, Davenport, IA*

WILST THOU MARRY ME?

$\mathcal{J}$ proposed to Melanie on a beautiful Sunday afternoon at the Renaissance Faire in Sterling, New York. But it almost didn't work out that way. The ring I had ordered hadn't arrived yet, so I thought I would have to wait for another time to propose. But as I was walking around the Faire, I noticed a cheap look-alike that would do the job until the other one came in. So I bought the $15 ring and I was set. Now, all I needed was a little help.

I was all decked out as a prince of the Renaissance period. The timing was just right. Melanie was running late, which was convenient because I still needed to enlist someone to help set the scene. Just then, the mayor of Warwick (the name of the Renaissance town the festival was set in) walked by. I approached him with my dilemma and he agreed to help out.

When Melanie appeared, I took her hand and started walking toward Lover's Bridge. As we approached, the mayor loudly proclaimed, "Here ye! Here ye! Lords and Ladies! I would like to introduce Lord Rodney and Lady Melanie for a most happy announcement!"

Melanie looked shocked and asked me how the mayor knew our names, but I just shrugged off her question. I escorted Melanie onto the bridge and we stopped at the Proposal Bench. I got down on one knee and proposed to Melanie. "Lords and Ladies, I ask of you to be witness to my proclamation of love for this woman, whom I have loved for the past year and a half."

By now, tears were flowing from our eyes. Melanie looked stunned. I continued, "What is this? For it is I who has butterflies in my stomach, fluttering like the wind. I shall love you and only you, this I proclaim. I ask you if thou wilst marry me?"

Melanie, still in shock and unable to say a word, simply nodded her head yes. But, of course, that wasn't enough for me. I wanted a verbal response. I said, "I need to hear the words, what say you? Wilst thou marry me?" Somehow, Melanie found the strength to speak. "Yes!" she cried.

And a cry of rejoice rang through the land as my fair maiden accepted my hand. The End.

—*Rodney Schmitz, Buffalo, NY*

A STICKY SITUATION

$\mathcal{B}$ecky and I had been dating for about four years, and I was in my last year of college. We had seriously discussed getting married and even went ahead and booked the church for a date two years down the road. In the meantime, I was saving up to buy her an engagement ring. Even though she knew when and where we were getting married, I wanted to propose to her in a very memorable way.

Just after we put down a deposit on the reception hall, Becky was sent to Zurich, Switzerland, for her job. A month later, she asked me to visit for a week and travel through Frankfurt, Amsterdam, and Paris with her. Then it hit me—Paris would be the perfect setting for my proposal! I bought her a beautiful diamond ring and mapped out my plan. I knew she would probably take charge of packing and repacking our bags, and I didn't want her to accidentally find the ring, so I wrapped it up tightly in a big ball of duct tape and shoved it in the bottom of my suitcase. Even if she found it, she would never think to unwrap it.

I arrived in Zurich and we had a blast. Midway through the week, we headed to Paris. On our second day there, we decided to go to the Eiffel Tower. It was time to put my plan into action.

That morning, while Becky was in the bathroom showering and brushing her teeth, I stayed in the other room. I pulled out my ball of duct tape and tried to unwrap it as quietly as I could. However, being in a small one-star hotel room, the bathroom door wouldn't close completely because the toilet was in the way. So, while she continued to talk my ear off, I snuck into the hallway to really put some strength into tearing the tape apart. Occasionally, I would stick my head into the room and say, "Umm hmm," so she would think I was really listening. I guess I didn't realize how hard I was pulling because as I pulled the last bit of tape off, the box opened and the ring went flying down the hallway. Unfortunately, at that moment the lights turned off (they do that in Europe to conserve energy) and I was forced to blindly crawl under a table in search of the ring. Lucky for me, I found it in just enough time to put it back in its box, slip it into my pocket, and step back into our room before Becky even noticed I was gone.

Because we were leaving Paris that night, we decided to check out of the hotel and leave our backpacks in a locker at the train station. In order to get to the lockers, we had to go through a metal detector. Becky went through without a problem, but I set the alarm off. I took off my watch, rings, and belt, but the alarm continued to sound. That's when I really started to panic. It was the metal in the ring box that was causing the problem! While Becky stood a few feet away, I tried to inconspicuously pull the ring out of my pocket to show the guard without letting Becky see it. By some stroke of international luck, the guard understood what was going on, despite the language barrier, and allowed me to go through the metal detector. What a relief! Fortunately, Becky had no idea what was going on.

We finally made it to the top of the Eiffel Tower. As we stood looking out at the beautiful view, I decided the time was right. I asked a girl standing next to us to take our picture. Just as she was getting ready to shoot, I took Becky's hand, dropped to one knee, and asked her to be my wife. She began to cry and shake and finally said yes. Every ounce of trouble I had gone through was well worth the smile on her face at that moment.

—*Daniel Thorkildsen and Rebecca Robak, Itasca, IL*

NUTS, CHEWS, AND DIAMONDS

𝒯o celebrate our three-year anniversary of dating, I took my girl-friend, Sharon, to the same restaurant we went to on our first date. Among the traits Sharon and I share is an insatiable appetite for sweets. During dinner, I suggested we go back home for a high-calorie, chocolate-filled pig-out, courtesy of yours truly. She happily agreed.

When we got home, we changed into our pajamas and sat in front of the fireplace, drinking a bottle of wine. We talked about all of our excellent experiences and accomplishments over the past year. Then it was time to exchange gifts. Sharon gave me a love poem and a collage of pictures of leather briefcases, so I could pick the one I wanted. After thanking her profusely, I jumped up and said it was time to eat dessert.

I went into the kitchen and returned with a long cake box and a wrapped present. I said that before she could open the present, we should try the dessert. She agreed and I lifted the box top. Instead of a cake, inside there was a shrink-wrapped box of Godiva Chocolate Truffles. I handed her the box and gave her the honor of unwrapping it and choosing the first one.

Excitedly, she took off the cellophane and opened the gold box. Her mouth dropped when she discovered what was inside. On each piece of chocolate there was a letter written in white icing that spelled out: "Will you marry me?" (Unfortunately, some of the icing stuck to the top of the box, so it actually read: "ill you marr me?") I quickly fixed it and watched as she followed the letters down to the bottom row where there was an arrow pointing to the very last hole.

Instead of a piece of chocolate, there was a diamond ring mounted in a small velvet box.

Sharon's eyes opened wide. Then she started to hyperventilate into the carry-out bag from dinner. I asked her if that was a positive or negative response and she screamed, *"Yes!"* She began to hug and kiss me. After she calmed down, she asked if she could open the other present. She did and was elated to find a bridal magazine to help her plan our wedding.

—Adam Layne, Farmington Hills, MI

TANGO FOR TWO

J thought long and hard about how to propose to Catherine. I consulted a lot of people—friends and family—for advice. Some of their suggestions sounded hokey, some sounded way too elaborate, while others sounded incredibly simple. In the end, I decided that my way was the best way.

I had my younger sister stake out the music department of a nearby university. Her mission was to find someone to play music while I swept Catherine off her feet and proposed. She saw a man walking with a classic jazz guitar. She introduced herself to him and told him about my idea. He loved the plan and even asked some other musicians to join his makeshift wedding proposal band.

We were like NASA planning a launch. Once the ring was ready, I called him and finalized our plans. Because it was necessary for everything to go perfectly, we went over every last detail.

At ten minutes after 6:00 P.M. on the agreed upon date, he was outside my front door waiting. I ran next door and begged my neighbors (who were in the middle of dinner) to get Catherine out of the house for five minutes. That was all the time we needed to put the plan in motion.

The musician and his two buddies quickly set up their instruments in the backyard—a jazz guitar, a saxophone, and a stand-up bass. I hurriedly put up a half-dozen tiki torches around our brick patio. My hands were shaking so much that the saxophonist had to help me light the torches.

The torches and band were ready. I was ready. But Catherine had not returned from the neighbor's house. After what seemed like an eternity, she arrived back at our house. I could read on her face that she knew something was up, but to her credit she played along. She could see the band through the window and asked who they were. Then she saw the tiki torches and walked into the backyard. On my cue, the band started playing "All of Me," and I asked her to dance. We slow danced the entire song as the smile on her face became bigger and bigger.

I didn't have a fancy ring box, so I had tied the engagement ring to a champagne flute and placed it on the edge of the patio. After the song, we walked to the patio. The saxophonist jumped the gun and asked Catherine if she had said yes. She replied, "He hasn't even asked me yet." We both laughed, and the saxophonist turned red with embarrassment.

Not letting this little gaffe stop me, I picked up the champagne glass with the ring attached. I turned to Catherine and asked her to marry me. She said yes, and we slow danced to our private band for another hour. We were married five months later, and the same trio played at our reception.

—*Barrett B. Blaum, New Orleans, LA*

B 9, N 36, I DO

*M*y boyfriend and I went on a cruise last February. On the second evening of our trip, we dressed up for "formal night." After dinner, we went to the showroom to watch that evening's entertainment. While we were waiting for the show to begin, we played bingo with the rest of the passengers. To my surprise, the cruise director selected my boyfriend to go up onstage to make sure all of the numbers were there.

After he checked the numbers, she looked at him and said, "I understand you would like to ask someone in our audience a question," and handed him the microphone. My boyfriend then asked me to join him on the stage. When I walked over to him, he got down on one knee, and in front of the one thousand people in the room, asked me to be his best friend and companion for the rest of our lives! I said yes and hugged him, and the audience burst out in applause. At that moment, I felt like the luckiest woman on the entire ship. It was better than any bingo jackpot I could ever have won.

—*Cyndi Reeves, Charlotte, NC*

THE SPIRIT OF CHRISTMAS

J decided to propose to Wendy Barbrie at Midnight Mass on Christmas Eve at St. Augustine's Church in Millville, Massachusetts. Each year for the past ten years that we've been dating (we were high school sweethearts), Wendy and I have traveled home for the holidays to attend this Mass with our parents. Because we don't get to see our families too often, I thought it would be especially poignant to propose in front of them, our friends, and God.

On December 23, I approached St. Augustine's pastor, the Reverend Jean-Paul Gagnon to let him know of my plans. Not only was he helpful, but he was also very excited. I couldn't wait for the next day and found myself becoming more and more nervous.

Finally, it was Christmas Eve and we went to Mass as planned. The big moment came when Reverend Gagnon was about to finish the Mass shortly after 1:00 A.M. He asked everyone to remain seated and to take a moment to reflect on love and the spirit of Christmas. Then he looked at me and I stood up.

I was sweating and shaking because Wendy and more than two hundred parishioners—including both sets of our parents—were staring at me. I faced the congregation and said, "Tonight I am here with the love of my life, Wendy Barbrie, the most beautiful and amazing person I have ever met. I thank God for giving her to me and allowing us to spend our days together." I then turned to Wendy and continued, "And so, on this very special Christmas Day before all of you, our parents, and God, I'd like to ask Wendy to be my wife."

When I took the ring out of my pocket, Wendy was shaking. I put the ring on her finger, and she said yes. The congregation started applauding. Several people had tears in their eyes. Father Gagnon called us to the front of the church and gave us a special blessing for the engaged.

On June 9, 1998, we were married at St. Peter's Basilica in Vatican City. The next day we were introduced to Pope John Paul II and received a special marriage blessing.

—Jay Faneuf, Los Angeles, CA

ONCE UPON A TIME

$\mathcal{I}$ don't have a story of my own to tell but I would like to share with you a story that has been a part of my family lore for years.

It began in the early 1900s. My grandfather, Lindsey Boyd Allen, went to Indian Territory (the current state of Oklahoma) as a young man. He had been trained as a blacksmith and made farm implements, wagon wheels, horseshoes, and the like. One day, while he was working, he noticed a beautiful young woman. Her name was Rachel and she was three-quarters English and one-quarter Chickasaw Indian.

One of my grandfather's favorite pastimes was to sing in the town's barbershop quartet. Well, he was so taken with Rachel that he and his friends would go over to her house and sing on her front lawn. Rachel's father, German Bartlett, was more than six-foot-four and very protective of his daughter. He would never let Lindsey onto the porch. So Lindsey spent many evenings out on Rachel's front lawn, proclaiming his feelings for her through song.

One Sunday afternoon, Lindsey passed by with a brand new buggy that he had just finished building the day before. He asked German if he could take Rachel for a ride. German replied, "So long as you don't go out of sight of the house." So my grandfather and Rachel left the yard sitting side by side for the very first time. In fact, the first time Lindsey ever touched Rachel was when he helped her into the buggy.

They rode a few hundred yards from the house and then back. Then they turned around and did it again. After the third circuit, he stopped well in view of the house and asked Rachel, "Would you like to see a picture of the girl I am going to ask to marry me?" She was crushed, but gamely smiled and said, "Surely."

My grandfather reached inside his coat pocket and pulled out a small leather photo wallet. The leather cover prevented her from seeing what was inside. He held it right in front of her, opened it, and there, instead of a photo, was a small mirror.

She stared at it for a long moment, and then said, "My father will hear of this." Neither of them said another word until they were back at her house. Lindsey asked German if he could come up onto the porch. German replied, "For only a few minutes." Lindsey stepped onto the porch, walked right up to German, and asked his permission to start courting. German sternly nodded his approval.

Lindsey and Rachel's courtship was carried out on the front porch or in the buggy—but always in view of the house. As the weather changed, Lindsey was permitted into the front parlor. One year later, they were married. They had never been alone together except when they had been in the buggy. The first time my grandmother and grandfather kissed was at their wedding.

—*Jon H. Allen, Winslow, AR*

THE BIG DIPPER

*S*uz and I had been dating for about two and a half years. We had only briefly looked at rings once, but she told me what type she liked, so I decided to surprise her on my own. After a lot of thinking, I decided to propose on the night before we were to leave on a sixteen-day vacation to Africa.

That evening, I cleared out my living room to make a big dance floor (this was the place where we first danced and kissed). I also put paper up all over the wall like a big canvas—we occasionally paint for fun—and placed wildflowers all around the room.

As an added surprise, I had picked up our favorite dessert, called "You Only Live Once Pie." We had eaten it almost once a week at a café that we used to go to when we first started dating. The restaurant closed about six months previously, however, so I had to track down the owner. After a little investigating, I discovered that he still worked in town at an import store. When I called, he remembered me and was happy to help me out. On the day of the big event, I stopped by the store and he took me back to his house, where he had one of the pies waiting for me in his refrigerator. It was well worth the search!

That night, Suz and I went out for dinner and returned to my apartment. I raced into the bathroom and took the ring out of its box. I had to hide it in a place that was easy to get to and where she wouldn't see it, so I wedged it under the waistline of my pants—not very romantic, not very comfortable, but it worked. I went back into the living room and asked her to dance. We danced for a bit and then, in the spot of our first kiss, I dipped her. When I lifted her back up, I had removed the ring and was holding it out for her. I dropped down on one knee and babbled a bunch of reasons why I wanted to marry her that were meant to be romantic, but I was so nervous I can't even remember what I said! She happily accepted my proposal and we danced a while longer. Then we turned our happiness into art as we painted with little kid paints using both brushes and our fingers. As we added the final touches, I took out the last surprise—champagne and the pie—which provided the perfect ending for such a memorable night.

—*Matt LeSage, Atlanta, GA*

A WALK IN THE PARK

as I watched him scraping the mud from his shoes, I fell in love with Scott. We had been dating for a while, but it was on this unusually warm February day in South Dakota's Cotton Park that I suddenly realized that this guy was different; this guy was special. I can't explain precisely why on this particular day I knew something had changed in our relationship, but love can be mysterious that way.

A year and a half later, Scott moved ten hours away. I still had one more year of college, so I decided to finish my schooling and then join him. It was a difficult time to say the least, but our relationship continued to thrive even though there were many miles between us.

Graduation day finally arrived, and Scott came to help me move. We decided to go for one last walk in Cotton Park and found a nice place by the river to stop and rest. Scott pulled a walkman out of the bag he had been carrying. He had rigged it up with two sets of headphones. As he put one set of headphones on me and the other on himself, he leaned in for a hug and we began to dance. The music he played was the theme from the film *The Princess Bride,* our favorite movie. There were tears in Scott's eyes as he sang the song to me while we danced.

When the song was over, we took off the headphones and stared deeply into each other's eyes. He said, "Well, that's about it, except . . . will you marry me?" He reached into his pocket and pulled out a ring. I burst into tears. I was so overwhelmed by this perfect day, this perfect proposal.

—*Jennifer Grouling, Des Plaines, IL*

ON THE TOWN

$\mathscr{H}$elen and I had been together for nearly a year. I knew she was the woman I wanted to marry. I also knew that I wanted my proposal to be romantic, unexpected, and memorable. I decided to propose the week before Valentine's Day. Because Valentine's Day was quickly approaching, Helen was becoming very suspicious of everything I said and did. I needed something to get her mind off the engagement idea.

I have clients in the chemical industry, so as a diversion, I decided to hold my own personal awards reception for the chemical industry at the New York Marriott Financial Center. Of course, this event never existed but Helen didn't know that. In early January, I sent Helen an e-mail asking her if she would be interested in going to the "Cocktail and Awards Reception" as my date. Sure enough, she took the bait. The fact that we would be attending a cocktail reception guaranteed that she would be dressed up for an evening on the town.

Friday, February 6, finally arrived! I left the office early. I went home, changed into my suit, packed up a bag of little gifts, and caught the New Jersey Transit train into Manhattan. From there I took a taxi to One If by Land, Two If by Sea, an eighteenth-century carriage house and restaurant located in Greenwich Village. I left the bag of gifts with the coat check and checked with the maître d' about my reservation and seating preferences.

After all of the restaurant arrangements were made, I took a taxi uptown to Helen's office to pick her up. Helen was still convinced that the evening was to consist of dinner and then the cocktail reception.

We entered the dimly lit restaurant, were greeted by the maître d', and then escorted up to the second floor to a small private table in front of a fireplace. There was a pianist, who delighted us with love songs and ballads all evening. When I placed my dinner order, I also put in the dessert order. Helen thought this was a little odd, but I explained that I was ordering chocolate soufflé and it requires thirty minutes' preparation time.

After dinner, I excused myself to go to the restroom. While I was away, I slipped the ring box to the waiter and told him to bring it out with the dessert. Dessert arrived and the waiter placed the soufflé on the table with the ring box positioned in front of Helen.

Her first reaction was "I knew it! I knew it!" as tears of joy filled her eyes. I quickly added, "You didn't know anything" (which she later admitted was true). Helen opened the box. I think she was pretty awestruck when she finally looked at the platinum and diamond engagement ring. I took the ring out of the box and placed it on her finger. I got down on my knees and asked her to marry me. She happily accepted. We ordered champagne and toasted the beginning of a wonderful evening and a wonderful life together.

The engagement adventure didn't stop there. I handed Helen a custom-made card, which I'd written and had printed at a local stationary shop. Inside the card were tissues to dab her tears, lottery tickets, a brochure on wedding bands, a listing of top wedding-related Web sites, and six business cards with ideas on what we could do after dinner.

While Helen was reading the card, I slipped out to the restroom again. I stopped on my way back to the table and picked up my bag of goodies from the coat check. Each gift was wrapped in paper with roses on it and ribbon that said, "I Love You" all the way around. She opened each gift in the order I had pre-determined.

First, there was a bottle of jewelry cleaner to keep her new "trinket" clean. The next package was a framed love message that I had picked up at a little shop we visited last year. She's a big Beanie Baby fan, so the third gift was the plush purple Princess Beanie Baby in memory of Princess Diana. Finally, the last box contained a Precious Moments "Say I Do" figurine.

After we finished our desserts, we caught a taxi uptown to the Empire State Building. We had gone there on our first date, so we thought it would be an appropriate place to visit on our engagement night. We took the elevator to the top to enjoy the romantic view of New York City on a cold, crisp evening.

After leaving the Empire State Building, we went to the Rainbow Room in the NBC Building. We enjoyed a bottle of champagne in a private corner booth, which overlooked the bar and had a view of Manhattan. We also danced on the revolving dance floor for a few minutes before leaving.

For our last event of the evening, we stopped by Central Park for a horse and carriage ride around the park. We snuggled under a blanket as the horse trotted through the park while the stars and city lights twinkled above us.

Unfortunately, though, all good things must come to an end. Around 1:00 A.M., we took our final taxi back to Grand Central Station so Helen could catch the last Metro North train home to Westchester. A quick goodnight kiss and the taxi continued on to Penn Station to drop me off for the last New Jersey Transit train home. It was definitely an evening we will always remember.

—*Michael Bielen, Westfield, NJ*

ROCKY MOUNTAIN HIGH

$\mathcal{M}$y boyfriend, Doug, took me up to Lake Agnes in Colorado for the weekend. It's a beautiful lake nestled on the mountainside surrounded by trees, flowers, and little waterfalls. After a great picnic lunch, he excused himself and disappeared down the hill toward the lake. He came back about fifteen minutes later and guided me down to a trail strewn with pastel pink rose petals. He smiled at me and said, "Will you follow the path to my heart?" I happily agreed.

The path led me past the lake's edge and up a small hill. At the top was a huge heart outlined by thirteen small glowing red candles and filled with more pink rose petals. On top of the petals were three different colored roses: red for love, white for purity, and pink for innocence. Next to the flowers was an envelope and a small box wrapped in heart-covered paper. Doug told me to open the envelope first. Inside was a poem entitled "Will You Take a Chance?" It was the most beautiful, romantic, and sincere poem I'd ever read and it made my heart melt. When I read the last line—"*Will you marry me?*"—I almost lost my balance!

I opened the box and discovered a gorgeous Cinderella-style diamond ring. I took a moment to let everything sink in and then said, "Yes." We hugged for a while and I kept thinking how lucky I was that this wonderful, romantic, sensitive man wanted to spend the rest of his life with me. A few minutes later, we walked back down the hill hand in hand, as future husband and wife.

—*Jennifer Muckala, West Covina, CA*

MUM'S THE WORD

Jason and I had been dating for six years and we had talked about marriage many times. We had even gone to look at rings. After I graduated from college, I had a sneaking suspicion that the day would come soon, but I was in the dark as to where, when, and how.

One day in September, Jason and I made plans to meet at his parents' farmhouse after I got off work. This was not unusual because we met there often. As I pulled up the long driveway, I noticed a big rainbow-colored hot air balloon in the yard. Standing around were Jason, his mother, father, sisters, brothers, and several farm hands. I hurriedly parked my car and ran over to where everyone was standing. As I approached, Jason's sister said, "You guys are going to go up first, then we're going to take a ride."

I was so excited! Giggling like a schoolgirl, I jumped into the basket. Everyone was pointing cameras at us and then up, up, up we went. I was speechless as I looked around—everything was so beautiful from that height. I could see for miles. Then Jason said, "Kristie, look!"

I turned around to look and there it was . . . "Will U Marry Me?" was written with 450 white mums in the middle of a field. Each letter was twenty feet tall. It was one of the most beautiful things I had ever seen. I screamed so loud that my future father-in-law heard me from down below. He remarked, "Well, I guess that was a yes."

—*Kristina and Jason Drift, Belle Mead, NJ*

MIDNIGHT SNACK

$\mathcal{M}$y boyfriend, Stephen, and I met on a Saturday in August in one of the most unlikely places to find your mate . . . or so my friends say. We met at a dance club in Palo Alto, California, called The Edge. I wasn't looking for a mate that night, but seeing his smile from across the room made me want to tear down walls to get to him.

We had our first date two days later and we hit it off magnificently well. On our third date, about a week and a half after we first met, Stephen turned to me and said, "You know, I can totally picture myself being married to you and being happy." Until I met him, I had figured that I was destined to be single because I was so darn independent. But at that moment, I had a change of heart. I replied, "You know, I feel the same way."

Six weeks later, Stephen came to pick me up from the Italian restaurant where I worked. He usually picked me up after work, so I didn't think anything about it. It had been a long, busy night, so I was ready to go home. When Stephen arrived, he said, "Mind if we stay and have a drink?" I figured he must have had a stressful day at work and needed something to help him relax. I said no, I didn't mind.

Instead of heading to the bar, he ushered me to a secluded table in the corner of the restaurant. I protested, saying, "I can't sit back here in my uniform. I'm a trainer and it wouldn't look good."

"Oh, don't worry about it." Stephen said. "Just take off your apron and your tie and no one will know."

I did as he suggested and we had our drinks. One of my coworkers came over and asked if she could sing for me. I started to suggest that she sing for Stephen because I heard her sing all the time, but before I could get word one out, she started singing "When I Fall in Love." Then, my manager came up and gave me a piece of my favorite dessert, tiramisu.

I hadn't noticed that Stephen had gotten up. He walked around the table until he was next to me and then got down on one knee. "Have you looked at your dessert very closely?" he asked. I looked, and there, nestled on a piece of chocolate, was an engagement ring. By now all my coworkers had gathered around. In front of my coworkers and the guests in the restaurant, Stephen declared his love for me and asked me to marry him. I could hardly get out a yes as I kissed him.

—*Karen Maher, San Ramon, CA*

I'LL HAVE A BURGER, FRIES, AND AN ENGAGEMENT RING

J met Lora at Burger King, where we both were employed. At the time, I wasn't looking for a relationship. However, she was such an engaging person, I decided to ask her out on a date.

During a break at work, Lora ordered a special sandwich (a broiler with ketchup and tomatoes). I made the sandwich and put an extra wrapper on it. The wrapper said, "Dinner and a movie?" She accepted, and we had a wonderful first date and continued to date seriously for four years.

I wanted to propose to Lora in a way she'd never expect nor forget. On Christmas Eve 1997, I asked her to meet me for lunch at the Burger King where we used to work. Before she arrived, I wrote my proposal on a sandwich wrapper and placed her engagement ring inside. I figured it worked when I asked her out on our first date, so maybe it would be just as magical the second time around. I instructed the Burger King employees to use that wrapper when she ordered her food.

The big moment arrived and I was very nervous. Lora didn't suspect a thing. She casually ordered her food, sat down with me, opened up the sandwich wrapper, and read it carefully. She was shocked, but managed to say, "Yes." Needless to say, Burger King holds a special place in our hearts.

—*Earl Farber, Hamburg, NY*

STEP RIGHT UP

*M*y boyfriend, Gilbert, and I were attending the Big E, an annual fair in Springfield, Massachusetts, with my fourteen-year-old daughter, Jillian, and my boyfriend's roommate, David. We were walking around and browsing in some of the small shops.

As we rounded a corner, my daughter spied a water balloon game where the prizes were stuffed Chihuahuas, like the dog from the Taco Bell commercials. Jillian was very excited and pleaded, "Can we play? Can we play?"

I gave in and decided I would play as well. To my surprise, I won. But the woman running the game said that I couldn't have one of the stuffed dogs. I was puzzled by this announcement. I was ready to argue when she said, "For today only, we have a special prize!" She held up a box that contained what looked like a beautiful diamond ring, but I thought it was a cheap imitation. I said, "I can't believe I'm getting a junky ring for a prize."

Gilbert turned to me and said, "Patty, take the ring. Look at it!" I looked closely at the ring and suddenly it dawned on me—it was an engagement ring. I was completely shocked.

Gilbert got down on one knee and asked me to marry him. Of course, I said yes. Incidentally, I did get my prize. Just the other day, Gilbert bought a miniature Taco Bell dog that says: "*Yo quiero Taco Bell.*" I keep it on my computer at work as a constant reminder of that wonderful day.

—*Patricia Amari, Boston, MA*

DOWN UNDER

*S*hortly after I graduated from college, I moved to a small town called Albury, about three hours northeast of Melbourne, Australia, to work for a pet food company. I immediately became involved with a group of people who, like myself, were recent recruits from college. A small group of us went camping one weekend and that is where I met Mark. We spent the next two and a half years traveling all over the world together.

One day, Mark picked me up from work. In the back of the car, he had stowed some packed bags. He told me that he had arranged for both of us to have Friday off. We were going to Sydney, his hometown, so I could spend the day shopping. I was thrilled with the fact that we would have a long weekend to spend together.

Friday morning, Mark drove me to my favorite shopping area in town. He hurriedly shooed me out of the car. He said that I could have the morning to myself and that he would meet me for lunch in a few hours. Unbeknownst to me, while I was trying on hats and shoes, Mark was out picking up my engagement ring.

We eventually met up for lunch. While we were eating, we discussed what we would do that evening. I suggested a romantic dinner at one of the best restaurants in Sydney. We had wanted to go there for ages but had never made it. Mark readily agreed (actually, he had already made reservations there).

The dinner was spectacular. After dinner, we decided to go for a walk along the Sydney Harbor. It was a rainy evening, so we snuggled underneath an umbrella as we walked. On a hill just by the water's edge, I stopped walking to take a moment and enjoy the beautiful view.

At this point, Mark started to act a little funny. He didn't want to stand still; he wanted to keep walking. He couldn't get me moving fast enough, so he proceeded to drag me down the wet, slippery hill to the sidewalk. Once we were beneath the bridge and sheltered from the rain, I climbed up to sit on the fence so I would have a better view of the harbor.

But Mark wasn't happy with that either. He pulled me off the fence and started dancing with me. He also began to sing "Champagne Supernova"—the song he sang to me the night we first fell in love. It was at this exact spot on the harbor more than two years earlier.

Suddenly, Mark stopped singing. He turned me toward him, got down on one knee, and said, "Chrissy, will you marry me?"

I think I must have said, "Oh my God" about a dozen times. He stood up, took my left hand, and slid a beautiful diamond engagement ring onto my finger. I threw my arms around him and finally managed to squeeze a "Yes!" out.

We chuckled and kissed under the bridge for another ten minutes before heading back to our B&B. When we got there, I saw a dozen roses on the dressing table. Next to the roses was an envelope. I looked at Mark and he had a funny smirk on his face. I asked, "What's this?" All he said was, "Open it and see." Inside were two tickets to go to Port Douglas on the Great Barrier Reef for seven days. What a guy!

—*Christine Scheer, Albury, Australia*

KIDS SAY THE DARNDEST THINGS

J have a seven-year-old daughter from my first marriage, and my boyfriend, Jimmy, has custody of his four-year-old brother. One Saturday afternoon, I noticed that Jimmy and the kids had spent a long time outside playing with the rest of the children in the neighborhood. I went out to see what they were doing and suddenly Jimmy said, "Let's go shopping." Nobody thought this was unusual and sudden except for me, but I agreed to go.

The mall is only five minutes away. During the short ride I kept asking him what was going on, but he just drove and made small talk. As we parked and got out of the car, the neighborhood children came running out of the glass doors leading to the stores of the mall. They were carrying flowers and were followed by their camera-toting parents. My daughter had a box in her hand and Jimmy's brother said, "Jimmy loves you." In unison, all of the neighborhood children said, "Will you marry Jimmy?" I looked over and Jimmy was on his knee looking up at me.

"Well?"

I kneeled down and said, "Yes!" and all of the children tackled us in the middle of the parking lot!

—*Irene Rivera, North Hills, CA*

WORTH THE WAIT

*M*y husband and I met for the first time in kindergarten, and it was love at first sight! When we graduated from kindergarten, Preston refused to have his picture taken unless he was sitting next to me, which is pretty dedicated for a five-year-old. We were friends all the way through sixth grade. However, when we went to junior high, we had different classes and went our separate ways. I still liked him, but he was very shy and, at the time, his first love was baseball. I wasn't going to sit at home and do nothing, so I dated other guys.

We led different lives until our paths crossed again our senior year of high school. At our high school, the custom was for a senior football player to ask the girl of his choice to be his maid on the homecoming court. On the day before homecoming, Preston walked into my homeroom. He asked me to be his maid, and I can't tell you whose face was redder, his or mine. I graciously accepted and wondered whether this would be the start of a more serious relationship with Preston.

We went to the homecoming dance and had a wonderful time. I felt that Preston and I had finally connected—that we were going to be "more than friends." But, much to my dismay, he didn't ask me to go out with him after that magical evening.

After we graduated from high school in 1962, he went his way and I went mine. I eventually married and had four children. Throughout the years, I would hear that Preston never married. Some people even said that he still cared for me, which was hard for me to believe.

Eventually, my first marriage failed, which was right around the time that I was working on our class reunion. I was organizing the event when Preston called to ask me if it was too late to RSVP. We talked for a while that day, and I told him that I was separated from my husband. He then asked me if I would go out with him. I didn't hesitate. The minute we saw each other, we knew that we belonged together. (By the way, he was still playing baseball.) Preston told me that he had always loved me. Over the years, he said he never felt the need to get married just because that was the proper thing to do—he was holding out for true love.

One night after having dated for several months, we were driving over the Greater New Orleans Bridge. When we neared the very top of the bridge, Preston turned to me and said: "Gayle, will you marry me?" My answer was a definite yes. He said that it felt like we were the only two people on the bridge that night. Maybe it wasn't the champagne, candles, and dinner type of proposal, but the years it took for us to get together made that moment one of the most special in my life. He didn't even have a ring to give me, but I didn't care. Our love for and commitment to each other made it so memorable.

A year later we were married, and we have a son together who is now fourteen years old. Preston has been a wonderful father to the four children from my previous marriage. He always says he has five children, not one. I feel so lucky to have such a wonderful man in my life. He is my husband, lover, and friend.

—*Gayle Grundmeyer, Covington, LA*

AHOY, MATEY

*M*y boyfriend always enjoyed sailing. We had talked about taking sailing lessons and even buying a boat together someday. One night, while out on his parents' boat, he gave me a model pirate ship. I thought it was cute and symbolic of the future sailing we had talked about.

I asked, "Why a pirate ship?"

"A pirate ship always has treasure on it," he said, pointing.

I lifted up the little flap, and there was a beautiful diamond ring! I couldn't believe what was happening. He asked me to marry him. I cried, "Yes" as I threw my arms around him and gave him a great big hug.

—*Alexandra Gojic, Wayne, NJ*

DELIVER ME

I met my fiancée, Mary Ellen, through a mutual friend. We were all attending a Sonia Dada concert. We hit it off immediately, and by the end of the show we were holding hands. For their encore, the band played "Deliver Me," which happened to be our favorite song. It was during that song that we had our first dance and our first kiss.

Fast-forward exactly one year. For our anniversary, I had planned a special and memorable weekend. I told Mary Ellen to pack an overnight bag. When she asked what kind of clothes she should bring, I told her to dress casual. I suggested that she might want to wear the dress she wore on the night we first met because it looked great on her.

Now, she thought we were driving to a little town a couple hours north of Columbus. While on the road, I intentionally made a couple of wrong turns and we ended up at the airport in the long-term parking lot. She looked at me and said, "Are you an idiot? Now you're going to have to pay to get out of here." My response was, "Well, if we're going to have to pay for parking, we might as well go somewhere." I pulled out some earplugs and a blindfold. Mary Ellen had no idea what was going on or where we were headed.

When we arrived in Phoenix, Mary Ellen was in heaven. She loves warm weather and we had talked about going out west for some time. I had booked a room at a romantic resort located at the base of Camelback Mountain. To my surprise, the clerk, who knew of my plan, had upgraded us to the Honeymoon Suite.

The next day was filled with sightseeing in the desert. Mary Ellen kept bugging me to drive up to Sedona, but I convinced her that I had plans for that evening in Scottsdale. She reluctantly agreed, and we hurried back to our room to change for the evening. Luckily, she had taken my hint and was wearing the same dress she had worn when we met 365 days earlier. I was also wearing the outfit I had worn the night we met.

We drove to the Rocking Horse Saloon, a very "country-looking" place. Mary Ellen didn't want to go in at first because we don't really care for country music. I finally convinced her to go in, and as we passed through the front door, she noticed a poster announcing Sonia Dada in concert. She was excited and said, "I wonder if they ever play here." Then, a lightbulb went off in her cute little head and she exclaimed, "Oh my God, are they here tonight?"

Yes, they were! After much research and many phone calls to the record company, their agent, and finally the club owner, I found out where they were playing and bought tickets. The place was jammed. I managed to make friends with a fun-loving group of people so we could share their table up front. I secretly told my new pals what I had planned and asked them if they would be willing to record the special moment with the camera and camcorder I had hidden in the car.

The night of drinking and dancing was going great, but I still didn't know exactly how I was going to pop the question. Then fate stepped in. I was running across the street to get some more film when I literally ran into Paris, the lead singer of the band. I quickly explained to him how we had met, how Sonia Dada had become a big part of our lives, and what I wanted to do.

Paris put a hand on my shoulder and said, "That's beautiful. What can I do for you?" I was dumbfounded. I said, "I don't know for sure, but 'Deliver Me' is our song. Can you play that song for us?" He said he'd go one better than that and call us up to the stage. I was psyched!

Then things started to go wrong. The opening act blew all the electricity in the club and had to finish their set "unplugged." That set the evening back thirty or forty-five minutes and cut off Sonia

Dada's encore, which was to be our song. As soon as the concert ended, I found Paris out back being mobbed by female admirers.

He looked up at me and asked, "We still doing this?"

"Oh, yeah." I replied. He pulled Scotty, the band's other lead singer, into the mix and we headed back to the table. Mary Ellen's face lit up when she saw us coming. When we reached the table Paris began to serenade her.

"Well, you met 'bout a year ago and things have been goin' well. But you'll be sending out invitations soon and hearing wedding bells . . . Oh, no, wait a minute. I think I'm getting a little ahead of myself. I think Cris has something he wants to ask you."

At that moment, with the remaining concert-goers in a circle around us, I dropped to one knee, pulled out my grandmother's ring, and said, "Mary Ellen, in front of God, the good people of Sedona, Arizona, and Sonia Dada . . . Will you marry me?"

She said yes, of course. She threw her arms around me, and as Scotty and Paris sang an a cappella rendition of "Deliver Me," we began to dance. Whenever we get the chance, we make it to a Sonia Dada concert.

—*Cris & Mary Ellen Ferrante, Bexley, OH*

WITH A LITTLE HELP FROM MY FRIENDS

$\mathcal{T}$his story began five years ago. I had just graduated from art school and took an advertising job in San Francisco. Unfortunately, I was living in Atlanta at the time, so I had to move away from my family and my girlfriend of four years, Ashley, who was still in college.

Two years later, I was driving down to Santa Cruz with my roommate, Steve, for a Saturday volleyball session. On the way, we passed this very steep cliff with the most wonderful view of the beach. We stopped and looked around for a while. It was so beautiful that I knew that this would be the place where I would someday propose to Ashley.

A year later, I was in Las Vegas with Ashley and our best friends, Jennifer and Scott, who had been dating six months longer than we had. Saturday morning, we awoke to hear Jennifer sniffling—Scott had just asked her to marry him. Before I could even react, Ashley was trying on Jennifer's ring and crying too. Scott winked at me as a reminder of a pact he and I had made in high school—that we would each ask our future wives to marry us while the other one was present. I knew then and there that it was time to start planning.

I had to figure out how to get everyone, including Ashley, out to San Francisco without being too obvious. She would be graduating from college the following spring, so a Thanksgiving proposal was sure to surprise her. I asked her to fly out to San Francisco for the holiday and subtly suggested that Jennifer and Scott come, too. She thought it was a great idea and the date was set.

I knew that I not only wanted to propose on the cliffs, but I also wanted to have the words written in the sand below. The cliffs were more than sixty-five miles away from San Francisco, so I would need Steve to help me. Timing would be crucial: Steve would have to get to the cliffs, rappel down to the beach, and do the actual writing in the sand before the tides washed it away. In the meantime, I had to convince the entire group to head south for the day in the middle of November.

Steve and I figured out that the group should arrive at the cliffs around 4:00 P.M., when the tide would be just right. We worked out the size, font, and placement of the letters (I am in advertising, after all), along with the travel time and miles between the cliffs and my apartment. Then we came up with an excuse for us to go down there. Near the cliffs, we saw a little restaurant that Scott could say a friend recommended to him. I jotted down the name. Then I worked on the last detail—a celebration party. Fortunately, my boss offered to have it at his loft on the evening of the proposal, so everything was set.

Thanksgiving rolled around and Scott, Jennifer, Ashley, and Ashley's best friend, Erin, finally arrived. The plan was set for Wednesday. Knowing that the group would take forever to get ready, I would aim to leave the house around noon and Steve was going to leave work early and head down to the cliffs at 2:00 P.M. We would arrive at the cliffs by 3:30 P.M. or so and everything would be ready. After the proposal, we would relax and then head to the party at 8:00 P.M. I couldn't have been more ready.

On Wednesday morning, for some strange reason, everyone was up at 8:30 A.M. and ready to go by 9:00 A.M.—not a good sign. Scott knew he was supposed to recommend the restaurant and not let the group leave the house any sooner than 11:00 A.M. So we all started talking about what we wanted to do and Ashley suggested going to Napa because she'd never been there.

Here's where Scott was supposed to say, "No, no, no. Let's go down to Santa Cruz to this great restaurant my friend suggested."

Well, he didn't. The idiot agreed with Ashley and was trying to get us all to go to Napa. I was ready to kill him, but at the last moment, he came through and said what he was supposed to. They all agreed to go to Santa Cruz instead of Napa, but unfortunately, it was only 9:30 A.M. I had to kill some time, so I drove everyone around to some of the sights of San Francisco. After they all started getting testy, I began the drive down to the cliffs, but I kept acting like I was getting lost and driving as slow as a snail.

When we finally reached the restaurant, it turned out to be a total dive. The group was hungry, which meant we had to look for another spot to eat. It was only 2:00 P.M., so I needed to draw the search out in order to give Steve more time to set everything up. We finally found another place and sat down inside. Once we ordered our lunch, I ran to the phone to check in with Steve on his cell phone—he was just leaving the city. I headed back to the table to make the meal last as long as I could.

After everyone was finished, I couldn't stall any longer, so we started to head for the cliffs. On the way, we stopped at the restaurant Scott was "referred" to just to see what it looked like on the inside. Basically, I needed another phone to check in with Steve again. Fortunately, he had just finished the writing in the sand. I rejoined the group and we drove across the street to the cliffs.

When we arrived, the girls got out of the car and started running up the small hill to the edge. Scott and I quickly grabbed the video camera so we could tape the proposal for our families. We raced to catch up with them before they reached the edge and finally caught up with them at the top. Ashley looked down and on the sand below saw a huge heart (the size of a small post office) with the words "Ashley, will you marry me?" written inside. She didn't say anything. Then it hit her. Jennifer and Erin were crying, Ashley was looking at me in shock, and Scott was still trying to find the eyepiece of the camcorder. Right at that moment, I dropped to one knee and asked Ashley to marry me. Then she said, and I quote, "I think I'm going to throw up," followed by "Yes, I will." Then she started to cry a little. As she began asking, "How did you write it?" and "How did you get down there?" Steve drove up and brought us a bottle of champagne. I then explained to Ashley everything that led up to that moment.

We headed back to the city where Ashley and I called our parents to tell them the good news. After the calls, we all got ready to go out and celebrate the occasion. I told her we were going by her favorite bar, but on the ride, we would stop by my boss's place to share the excitement. We parked the car and walked to his front door. When the door opened, Ashley was shocked yet again to find all of our friends gathered there to celebrate our engagement. The smile on her face as she hugged me was the perfect touch to one of the greatest days of my life.

—*Michael Lewis, San Francisco, CA*

WHEN YOU WISH UPON A STAR

*T*ony, my boyfriend of two years, and I planned a trip to Disney World because it's his favorite place on the planet. I thought he was just a kid at heart, but I soon learned that he was also a true romantic. He had decided that the Magic Kingdom would be a magical place to propose.

On the night we arrived, we headed into the park and rode some rides. He told me that more than anything, he wanted to see the fireworks over Cinderella's castle at 9:00 P.M. At 8:45, we headed toward the castle. I spied a prime viewing place and grabbed it, but Tony said he wanted to see if he could find a better spot. He took me to a roped off area in the rose garden next to the castle. He told me that this was one of the "white glove" benefits we received by paying with our American Express card.

He led me to a spot where I was surprised to see a romantic setup—roses, chocolate truffles, champagne, and a love seat (still, I didn't clue in). I sat down and instead of sitting next to me, Tony got down on one knee (I clued in). I don't remember half of what he said because I was in shock. After his proposal, everyone around the perimeter of the garden broke out in applause. Just then Tinker Bell flew out of the castle and the fireworks began. We had the best view, and there were three Disney employees taking our picture, filling our glasses, and making us feel like royal guests of honor. It took hours for me to stop shaking!

—*Meg (Tobin) Sacchetti, North Reading, MA*

A GRADE-A PROPOSAL

J am a middle school teacher and my fiancé, Jeff, is a student at Bowling Green University in Ohio. We had been dating for two years when, to my surprise, he decided to pop the question.

One Wednesday morning in May, I was summoned to the office for a phone call. I hurried to the office, not wanting to leave my class unsupervised for too long. The caller was a colleague of mine wanting to ask me some questions about summer school. I was thinking, "Why couldn't this have waited until lunch?" The conversation seemed to take forever. When it finally ended, I hurried back to my class.

When I returned to the room, my students were standing in a semi-circle in the middle of the room, guilty expressions on their faces. I was irked, thinking they had been goofing off while I was gone. Then, one by one, each of my students walked up to me and handed me a red rose—all thirty of them!

I had no idea what they were up to. I heard a commotion at the door. I turned around and there stood Jeff. He was wearing a white tuxedo and holding three white roses: one for me, one for him, and one for God. By now, the hallway was filled with students and teachers. The principal was even there, videotaping the event.

Jeff got down on one knee and told me that he loved me and wanted to spend the rest of his life with me. He then asked for my hand in marriage. Of course I said yes. I thought the roof was going to cave in, the din was so loud from all of the cheering and clapping.

—*Amy Kinkle, Van Wert, OH*

DANCE WITH ME

I dance country-western ballroom style and was in a local dance competition a few years ago. Some mutual friends brought their friend Debbie along to help cheer me on at the event. That night Debbie and I danced for the first time—it was amazing. Over the next several months, I taught Debbie the basics of country-western ballroom dancing and we became close friends.

We were so compatible on the dance floor that I parted ways with my previous dance partner. Debbie and I began to train for a competition the following year. While we trained, our friendship grew into love and a strong relationship beyond the dance floor.

Before a competition in South Bend, I began to work on a unique way of popping the question to Debbie. I bought the ring and picked it up right before we were to leave for the event. I had decided to propose after we competed because I didn't want to make her nervous during our performance. After the awards ceremony at the end of the competition, I told Debbie that Dawn, our coach, needed our assistance in videotaping some dance moves.

We walked down a large, straight staircase that opened onto the lower level of the South Bend Century Center. It was a huge, completely empty room. There was a large window on one side of the room. When you looked out this window, you could see the river that runs through town and its waterfall. It was night, and the lights that illuminated the waterfall added a warm, romantic hue to the dimly lit room. In the background, we could hear the music from the ballroom. I couldn't have asked for a better setting.

But there was business still at hand. Dawn demonstrated a move with Debbie. I said, "Hey, I know that move! Let me try it!" I gave the camera to Dawn, who started videotaping the scene as I walked over to Debbie. I gazed at her and thought, *this is the last moment that Debbie will be thought of as my girlfriend.*

I reached deep into my pocket for the ring that had been there all day long. I went down on one knee in front of her. I was speechless. All I could do was hold the ring up to her. She slowly realized what I was trying to say and began to cry. She took my hand and came down on the floor to hug me. We both cried for about a minute, kneeling on the floor of this vast hall where we had taken several dance classes in the past. I placed the ring on her finger. We kissed, and then I motioned to Dawn, who was also crying, to turn off the camera.

We rejoined the party in the ballroom and let all of our friends in on the secret. Someone told the disc jockey that we had just become engaged. He made an announcement and played a special waltz to commemorate the occasion. The song, "You Make the Moonlight So Bright," became our song, and we choreographed a dance to it as entertainment at our wedding.

—*Scott Schuman, Pewaukee, WI*

FLYING HIGH

*M*y boyfriend, Ryan, and I went to Pomona, California, to see the drag races. We do this every year with his family and always have a lot of fun. We arrived around 8:00 A.M., met up with our friends, and took our seats.

Around 11:45 A.M., I wanted to go get a beer. Everyone kept telling me to wait and we would all go down together. I was starting to get a little impatient, though. So I got up and was ready to head out when Ryan's sister offered me the rest of her beer.

At that moment, a plane was flying overhead. It kept flying in circles right above us. I looked up and attached to the back of the plane was a banner that read, "Kim, will you marry me? Love, Ryan." I looked over at Ryan, and he was down on one knee right there in the grandstands. Everybody around us was yelling and cheering so much, I didn't quite hear what Ryan said, but I said, "Yes!"

—*Kim Meyers, Fresno, CA*

WITH THIS RING

*M*y boyfriend, Todd, and I were visiting Washington, D.C. We had a nice dinner with champagne in our hotel room, but we were both feeling a little restless just sitting around inside. Around midnight, we decided to go for a walk. We went to the Washington Monument, which was lit up beautifully, then we sat down on a bench to talk.

We both wanted to see where things stood between us and where they could go. We started talking about our future and, before we knew it, we had the rest of our lives planned out. Sitting right there under the Washington Monument, Todd asked me to marry him. Of course I said, "Yes!"

Because it was so spur of the moment, Todd didn't have a ring. Instead, when we got back to our hotel room, he found the gold twist-tie from the bottle of champagne and slipped it on my finger. I wore that twist-tie for an entire month before I got a new ring. I even had to tape and staple it together a couple of times to keep it on my finger.

I still have the twist-tie ring. I keep it in the box my diamond engagement ring came in. It means just as much to me as the other one does, and I plan to hand it down to our children someday.

—*Robyn and Todd Pollman, St. Petersburg, FL*

ON THE RIGHT TRACK

*J*im and I had been dating on and off for three years. It was steady at times, but after he went into the army, I began to date other men. However, deep down I always knew Jim was the one for me.

That fall, Jim came home, but by that time I was seeing a nice fellow named Bob, whose father owned a bakery. Fortunately for Jim, Bob was in the Marines and was out of town quite often. One October night, as Jim and I were driving to my brother's home for dinner, he stopped the car right on the railroad tracks in our village. He looked at me, tossed a small box in my lap, and said, "Now you can tell that loaf of bread to get lost!" I replied, "May I write Bob one last letter?" His answer was "Definitely." As I said yes to Jim's unusual proposal, he slipped the ring onto my finger. I was ecstatic and thought my tiny diamond was the greatest!

We have now been married forty-four years. Looking back on that evening, I really think he acted the way he did because he was afraid I'd say no.

—Vivian Fellows, Homer, NY

WHAT, THIS OLD THING

*M*y fiancé, Daniel, is always teasing me about being a princess. I have to admit, I did tell him once that if we ever got engaged, I wanted a big ring. His proposal was designed to truly test me.

We had been having a long distance relationship for three years. He'd recently moved to Charleston, South Carolina, and I was attending school in College Park, Maryland. I had just finished a series of big exams and decided to take a break and go visit Daniel. On my first night in town, we went to a fancy restaurant in the historic district of downtown Charleston. We arrived at the restaurant too early for our reservations, so Dan suggested a walk along Waterfront Park, a pretty walkway overlooking the water.

As we walked out toward the end of the main pier, he kept talking about our future. Finally, I asked, "What is with you? You never talk about stuff like this." He stopped walking, turned to look at me, and said, "I love you. Will you be my wife?"

Because he hadn't really led up to the proposal (no ring, no getting down on one knee), it took me a few seconds to realize that he had proposed! I happily said yes, but I was still in shock. Then Dan pulled a ring box from his pocket. When he opened the box, I saw the tiniest diamond I had ever seen.

As I stood there staring at the ring, he told me he was sorry he couldn't afford a really nice ring because he had just bought a house. But, he assured me, we could exchange it for a bigger one when he could afford it. Not knowing what else to say, I replied, "Yeah, sure, I'll trade it in for a bigger one."

As soon as the words were out of my mouth, I regretted saying them. Dan had once told me that he couldn't understand why people felt the need to upgrade their engagement rings. He explained that the rings were representative of the couple as they were starting out. At the time, I had agreed, but quickly added that additional jewelry could be purchased as the couple progressed financially.

So, as I was standing on the pier with that speck of a diamond being held in front of me, I said to my future groom, "No, this is the ring you proposed to me with and this is the one I want to keep forever!" Dan stepped back from me and said, "Good answer!" Then he tossed the ring up into the air. It went over the edge of the pier into the water. I was shocked speechless.

"How about this ring?" he asked, as he pulled the most beautiful ring I have ever seen from his pocket. He then said that he could tell I liked it by the way my eyes seemed to pop out of my head. Incidentally, the first ring was just a cubic zirconia.

—*J. Kish, Goose Creek, SC*

SUPERMARKET SWEEP

$\mathcal{T}$erry and I both grew up in Los Angeles and went to college in Denver. During one of our breaks, we drove out to Los Angeles from Colorado to visit our parents. After a great week, it was time for us to drive back. I was at the market with my mom buying road munchies, when she was paged by my dad. She went to the pay phone to call him, and when she came back she was laughing hysterically. When I asked what was so funny, she said nothing and kept on laughing. She finally told me that my dad had told her a joke. I blew it off and continued down the aisles.

After we finished shopping, I dropped my mom off and went to pick up Terry. I was wearing a T-shirt and boxer shorts and I had not showered because we were going to be driving for the next sixteen to eighteen hours. When I arrived at his house, the door was locked, which it never is, so I rang the bell. I heard Terry's mom scream for him to answer the door, which also seemed weird. I wondered why she didn't get up and open it herself. Terry finally answered the door wearing a tuxedo, baseball hat, and tennis shoes. I was a little confused, but suddenly realized what was happening. He got down on one knee and said, "I love you, Jewlz. Will you marry me?" As I excitedly said yes, he opened up a black velvet box with a sparkling solitaire diamond ring inside and the rest is history.

It turns out the page my mom got was my dad telling her that Terry had called him up to ask if he could marry me! My mom was so excited, she couldn't control herself.

—*Julie Fahn, Pacific Palisades, CA*

LOVE THE SECOND TIME AROUND

*a*s a divorcée with two young girls, I found that I wasn't meeting many men. To improve this situation, I placed a rather sarcastic Internet personal ad that said my idea of hell is an afternoon of touch football with the Kennedy clan.

The first day my ad appeared, I received a response via e-mail from David, a divorced father of two boys. David and I had many things in common, including our disdain for sports. We started dating, and after one month we knew we were in love.

Shortly after declaring our love for one another, we discussed getting married. I told David that my ex-husband had never really proposed, and I hoped my next proposal would be charming enough that I would relate the story over the years. To clarify further, I told him that taking me to an expensive restaurant where I find my dinner plate features a lobster with a diamond ring dangling from one claw was *not* my definition of a good story. David was silent.

A couple of weeks later, he asked me to walk with him to a park across the street from the small apartment that he shared with his sons. He said that he had a good friend in the horse and carriage business who was going to give us a carriage ride as a romantic surprise. Before the horse and carriage arrived, however, he blurted out, "Holly, I just can't wait. Will you marry me?" I pounced on him and exclaimed, "Yes, of course. And even without the horse and carriage, this makes a great story."

—*Holly Barrington, Monrovia, CA*

RUB-A-DUB-DUB

*M*y boyfriend, Harry, and I were in the process of remodeling the home we shared. One afternoon, I decided to unwind by taking a relaxing bath in our newly remodeled bathtub. I had painted and wallpapered the bathroom the day before, so the smells were still quite strong. As I settled into the bath, Harry opened the door to air out the room. He walked right over to me, knelt beside the tub, and said, "You'd sure make a good wife." I said, "Is this a proposal?" He answered, "Yes, I'd never be able to find anyone else who would know how to put grout between the tiles!" So, due to the remodeling of the bathroom, I was proposed to in the bathtub—and that's the truth!

—*Joanne Gillette, Syracuse, NY*

A WEST SIDE STORY

$\mathcal{I}$ met Annabel in an introductory psychobiology class at UCLA. After some study sessions together, I got up enough nerve to ask her to see one of my favorite movies, *West Side Story*, which was playing on campus at the Ackerman Grand Ballroom. The evening went remarkably well, and for seven years we were inseparable.

When it came time to propose, I knew there was only one place to do it: the Ackerman Grand Ballroom. Waiting for an open night at this venue proved to be a challenge, but I persevered.

To lure Annabel to campus and not arouse her suspicions, I told her that my cousin was shooting an Internet advertising spot and wanted us to be in it. When we opened the double doors at the back of the pitch-black ballroom, a big blue screen toward the front became visible. As we walked up the center aisle, past rows of empty seats, our favorite scene from *West Side Story* began to play. "Only you, you're the only one I'll see, forever," sings Maria to Tony in the film.

We sat in the same seats we had on our first date. I pulled a box of Red Vines licorice out of my pocket—we had eaten this candy on that fateful night. At the end of the song, I asked her to examine the Red Vines' box more closely. When she did, she discovered a beautiful engagement ring inside it. I kneeled before her and asked for her hand in marriage. With tears in her eyes, she told me softly, "Of course." And we proceeded to watch the rest of the movie in the peace and quiet of this truly grand ballroom.

—*Ken Hom, Canyon Country, CA*

SHELL SHOCKED

$\mathcal{D}$onna and I had been together for nearly six years. We had a very strong relationship and knew we were going to get married someday.

A few months ago, we purchased a brand new loft in downtown Toronto. This was an exciting step for us, but there was something about it that made Donna uncomfortable. What troubled her was the fact that we were making all these great plans for our future, yet we were not officially engaged. I apologized to her for getting ahead of ourselves and asked her to be patient for several months. I needed time to save up some money so I could afford to buy an engagement ring in order to propose to her formally.

Donna's birthday is in mid-May, so I felt the best way to propose to her was to surprise her under the guise of that occasion. I did not have much time to plan, so I cashed in all of the stocks I owned and bought her a beautiful diamond ring. I couldn't picture myself proposing to her in Toronto, however, because I wanted it to be something more memorable and more romantic—something that she would never forget.

It finally occurred to me what to do. The day before her birthday, I told Donna to pack because we were going for a long drive for her birthday. She was shocked when we arrived at the airport. "Where are we going?" she asked curiously. I told her it was a surprise and not to ask too many questions.

It was only when we checked in at the airport that she discovered we were going to Florida. She was very excited and wanted to know why we were going there. I told her, "Because we bought the loft, we really have to start saving our money, but I wanted to make this birthday really special for you. Because we have such a large financial responsibility coming up, consider this the last crazy, extravagant thing we do." I said it with such sincerity that she had no idea I had other motives.

We went to St. Petersburg on the Gulf coast of Florida. It was absolutely beautiful. Initially, I was planning to propose to her on the beach by the water under one of Florida's legendary sunsets. However, this is not exactly how it occurred.

At her suggestion, we decided to go to the beach to catch the sunrise. It was still fairly dark when we sat down on the sand. The sky was just starting to lighten up, but the sun had not broken the horizon. We sat there for several minutes just soaking in the serenity and beauty of the ocean. With the birds chirping up above and the surf gently crashing on the shore, it sounded like a hypnotic symphony. The romance of the moment was undeniable. I knew at that moment that I had to propose to her right there and then.

I excused myself and told her I was going to find her some seashells. Because it was early morning, the shore neatly displayed thousands of tiny treasures, but I took a few minutes to find a couple of choice specimens. I headed back to Donna and sat down beside her to proudly show off my bounty. She smiled in appreciation as she accepted my gifts from the sea. Little did she know, I saved the prettiest one for last. I placed the tiny shell on the third finger on her right hand as if it were an engagement ring. With a smile, I lightheartedly asked if she would marry me. She smiled in return, thinking I was just playing around, as I often do, and said, "Of course, I will marry you, but you have the shell on the wrong hand."

I apologized and reached into my pocket. With trembling hands, I slipped the real engagement ring on the third finger of her left hand. My mind was spinning and my heart was pounding. I had originally thought out what I wanted to say, but for the life of me

I couldn't remember it at that moment. It didn't matter anymore, so I just said what was in my heart. I gazed deeply into her eyes and simply asked, "Will you marry me?"

Donna was stunned. I will never forget the look of unabashed joy on her face. I don't even remember if she said yes, but the embrace she gave me was all the answer I needed.

—*Mark Guinto, Toronto, Ontario, Canada*

MOONLIGHT SURPRISE

*M*y boyfriend and I met more than five years ago down at the shore on Memorial Day weekend. We clicked from the moment our eyes first met. I believe that we were meant to be—he's my soulmate and I'm his. After four years of dating, I started to drop hints every now and then about marriage, but he never said a word.

Last year on Labor Day, we went away for a long weekend to the Catskill Mountains in New York, as we had done every summer. It was late at night and we were sitting in the outdoor Jacuzzi sipping wine and watching the stars—a truly romantic evening. Once we finished the bottle of wine, he volunteered to go back to the room to get another bottle. Before I could say, "Don't bother," he was gone.

He came back with the wine, a CD player, and a CD. He put on our song—"Can't Help Falling In Love with You" by UB40—and filled the wineglasses. I felt very moved by this romantic display. It seemed like such a perfect evening; I never imagined that my sweetheart could make the night even more memorable. Sitting on the edge of the Jacuzzi, he said, "Honey, we've got the stars, we're at our favorite summer spot, our song is playing, and I love you very much." As he said this, he reached into the pocket of his shorts and took out a small box and opened it. It was the most beautiful ring I had ever seen! I couldn't believe this was happening. Then he said, "Will you marry me?" I said, "Yes" and we hugged and kissed and time seemed to stand still.

He had planned this for months, waiting for the perfect time. I can't imagine a more perfect time or a more magical proposal.

—*Carla Da Silva, Newark, NJ*

LEAVING ON A JET PLANE

*O*ur relationship started online two years ago. He was getting over a bad relationship, and I had just ended a bad marriage. We both needed a friend and went online hoping to find just that. At first we were friends, but after talking online every single night until the morning hours, our relationship soon became so much more. There was only one problem: This guy, who was so perfect for me, lived 2,300 miles across the country. I knew I had to meet him, though, so last year I flew him out here to spend the week with me and my three children.

When I went to the airport to pick him up, I was so nervous I hid in a phone booth. Instead of giving him an open-armed greeting when he got off the plane, I snuck up behind him. I put my arms around him and told him not to turn around. I then instructed him to close his eyes and keep them closed. I led him over to a corner and planted a big kiss on him. I wanted to do this before he saw me just in case he didn't like what he saw.

Then came the moment of truth. He had to see me at some point. I told him he could open his eyes. He did and what happened next is what made me know without any doubt that I loved this man. He placed his hand on my cheek, lifted my chin up, looked me dead in the eyes, and said, "You're beautiful!" There were tears in both of our eyes. All I could say was, "I love you very much."

His visit went wonderfully well, but with every beginning there comes an end. The hardest thing I ever had to do was watch him walk away as he boarded the plane to go home. I vowed right then and there not to give up. Somehow I was going to make this relationship work. We might live apart now, but if I had anything to do with it, we wouldn't for long.

Since we had actually met, the online chats just weren't enough. So we started talking on the phone. We talked all day and all night, usually until I fell asleep on the phone (that's why he calls me his "sleeping beauty").

Finally, after $3,000 in phone bills, it was time for *my* visit. I bought myself a plane ticket to visit him for a week around Thanksgiving. When I got off the plane, he was waiting for me at the gate. I was just as nervous as the first time we met, but my desire to hold him in my arms again beat out my anxiety.

Every day that I was there he gave me a different card, each one romantic and unique in its own right. The day after Thanksgiving he gave me this card with two little kids on it, a boy and a girl. The little boy was holding a rose. Inside he had written:

"A million words could never say all I need to tell you, all I need you to know. Even if I could find the words that just won't come to me, they wouldn't be enough for all that you are to me. I love you Rosie and I want to share the rest of my life with you. Can I keep you, Rosie?"

Then, at the bottom in parentheses it said, "Look at me." I looked up and, with tears in his eyes, he said, "Will you marry me?" I cried so hard I could barely talk, but I did manage to get out a quick "Uh-huh."

—*Rosie and Rocky Hunter, Shirley, MA*

APRIL FOOL'S

*I*t was the first of April and my three-year-old daughter and I were spending a quiet day at home. My boyfriend, Tony, dropped by at lunchtime. The three of us sat and chatted, and then he brought up the subject of marriage. My heart started pounding at the thought of what might happen next. He pulled out a small black velvet box and asked, "Will you marry me?" I smiled and enthusiastically shouted, "Yes!" I opened the box, and to my surprise, inside was a big pink plastic ring.

Tony started laughing hysterically and said, "April Fool's!" I was angry, yet slightly amused that I had been fooled. After I calmed down, he took my daughter's hand and asked, "Taylor, will you marry me?" She grinned as she said yes, placed the ring on her finger, and began running around the apartment screaming, "I'm getting married!"

Then Tony looked at me, pulled out another black velvet box, and opened it, revealing a gorgeous, real diamond ring. Looking directly into my eyes, he caressed my hand and asked me again, "Will you marry me?" I smiled and politely said, "No." He looked shocked and closed the box. As his gaze dropped to the floor, I laughed and said, "April Fool's!" I immediately gave him a hug and kiss and said, "Yes." As his spirit quickly returned, we laughed together knowing that our humor would always be a binding force between us. We three were married that October.

—*Tresserlyn Lawson Jones, Newport News, VA*

HAPPILY EVER AFTER

*M*ike and I had been dating off and on for nine years. For the last two years, we had been discussing marriage, but after a lot of talk and no action, I had virtually given up on the thought of us ever saying "I do." Mike is a simple guy and I can read him quite easily. After nine years, I didn't think he could surprise or shock me, but he did the night he proposed.

During the first week in February, I found out that my brother, Troy, would be in San Diego with the touring ice skating show he was starring in, "Disney on Ice—Happily Ever After." He and I had been skating our entire lives and competing together for about fifteen years. Soon after I stopped skating, he joined the show playing the lead role of Hercules. Whenever the show was in town or nearby, I tried to see it. Mike and I live in Los Angeles, so driving two hours to see my brother wasn't too much trouble. We got a group of friends together and made plans to head south for the show that Saturday.

Unfortunately, right before we were supposed to leave town, Mike called and sadly informed me that he was stuck at work and wouldn't be able to come with us. He's a workaholic, often spending his weekends in the office, so this wasn't too surprising. With a little persuasion, he said he would try to meet us after the show for a party Troy had invited us to. I left it at that and my friend, Debbie, convinced me that a "girls' night out" would be just as much fun. I agreed. We rounded up the girls and hit the road.

At 7:00 P.M. we arrived at the arena and picked up our tickets. Troy had reserved two seats for Mike and me in the front row, with the rest of the seats a few rows behind. I was bummed that Mike couldn't be there to appreciate such great seats, but Debbie offered to sit with me as my "date" for the night.

Once we sat down, I pushed all thoughts of Mike aside and we had a blast during the first half of the show. Intermission began and we got up to stroll around. Only a few minutes had passed when the lights suddenly went dim again. Thinking that intermission was a bit too short, we quickly took our seats.

Unexpectedly, Troy skated out onto the ice, dressed in street clothes, with a bouquet of flowers and a microphone. Debbie asked me what was going on as Troy began to introduce himself. I shrugged and said, "Who knows. They always do out-of-the-ordinary things at these shows."

It wasn't until Troy began to give a speech that I realized this was something much more personal than any other event I had seen during his shows. He said, "Tonight I would like to honor a special member of the audience—someone I love, someone who has always supported me, and without whom I wouldn't be who I am today. She has been my partner throughout my life . . ." At that point, I was convinced he was honoring his wife, who was sitting in the audience, and thought it was sweet. As I looked over to her, I didn't realize that Troy had skated over to the ice right in front of me and I heard, "My sister, Dawn Goldstein." I turned around in shock and whispered to Debbie, "What is he doing?" She shrugged and urged me to stand up.

I walked up to him with a strange grin on my face, which was a combination of confusion and embarrassment. I hugged him and tried to forget about the five thousand people applauding us. I also noticed two cameramen to my left and thought how cool it was that Troy had arranged to capture the moment on video. Suddenly, Troy said, "However, these flowers aren't from me. They are from another very special member of our audience." I was very confused, then thought, *No way!* I turned around to see Mike bounding through the audience, heading right toward me. I was stunned.

He said, "Sorry I'm late," and took my hands in his. Troy placed the microphone in front of him, so everyone in the arena could hear the beautiful words he had to say.

"Dawn, you are the world to me. You are my sky, my air, and my earth. You are my sweet spring morning and my warm summer night. You are the bright autumn colors in my life. You are my best friend and I want to spend the rest of my days with you."

He got down on one knee, opened up a white box with the most gorgeous diamond ring inside, looked up at me, and said those words I had been longing to hear from him, "Dawn, will you marry me?"

I was absolutely shocked. My eyes got teary and I had the biggest smile on my face. I said, "Yes" softly to Mike, then a microphone was placed in front of me and I yelled it again for all to hear. Everyone clapped and the love song from *Cinderella,* "This Is Love," began to play over the loudspeakers. Mike then placed the ring on my finger. I was beaming. I hugged him like I never wanted to let go, but finally did so I could hug Troy. Debbie jumped up and hugged me, too. Then she winked at Mike and I shook my head in amazement. She told me that she had known about it for three weeks!

Suddenly, a woman with a microphone handed me another bouquet of roses and I noticed that the cameramen were still filming us. The woman smiled and said, "Congratulations, Dawn. In addition to being proposed to in front of five thousand people, you're also on national television on *Inside Edition.* How do you feel?" I couldn't speak, but somehow managed to answer all of her questions about my engagement. Then we all sat down to watch the second half of the show, but I couldn't stop grinning at Mike or staring at my beautiful ring.

It turns out that for several weeks, Mike, Debbie, and Troy had been masterminding this perfect and romantic proposal for me as part of a Valentine's Day story for the entertainment news show *Inside Edition*. I couldn't believe they kept such a big secret from me! But I'm so glad they did. It couldn't have been a more perfect proposal creating a memory that I'll never forget.

—*Dawn Goldstein, Los Angeles, CA*

A GRAVE PROPOSAL

We traveled 12,000 miles from Melbourne, Australia, to Whitby, England (a wonderful small village), on Halloween so that we could attend the Whitby Gothic Weekend. It was the perfect setting for what I had planned.

As with all Gothic evenings, it started out with the makeup. We both laughed and danced as we put on four layers of foundation, powder, and eyeliner, and dressed in our best French lace, thick (and thankfully very warm) capes, and leather boots. We had a few sips of our favorite wine and swayed about the room to the music of the Baroness, a Gothic recording artist. We hugged each other, and then headed out arm-in-arm to face the night.

We headed toward the intoxicating beat of a Gothic dance club—one of the first events of the weekend. Hugging closer, we entered and were soon compressed into a very, very small space with six hundred other Goths. We had never been so filled with a sense of belonging. The blissful evening was full of strange and exotic encounters with the most delightfully friendly Goths, but by 12:30 A.M. we had sated our appetite for frenzied dancing and I knew that it was my time.

I said cryptically to my beautiful Gothic lover, "We have far to go." We walked back to our hotel. I was breathless with anticipation; my lover was oblivious to what awaited her. I went up to our room and retrieved an excellent red wine that I had secreted away (all the way from home), and we headed back out into the night.

We walked through the narrow streets toward an abbey on top of a cliff overlooking a black sea. We climbed the 199 steep steps and we were there—not quite the abbey, but an ancient graveyard that is at the top of the cliff. It was the perfect place to proclaim my love. There we stood in a graveyard at 1:05 in the morning of Halloween, clutched tightly together for warmth. I then asked my lover to be mine. She looked at me and said yes. She accepted my dark love and returned it in kind.

—*Paul Rawson, Melbourne, Australia*

LET THEM EAT CAKE

*M*y boyfriend and I were vacationing in the Poconos to celebrate our second anniversary of dating. On the first evening of our vacation, we ate dinner at the resort's restaurant. Dinner was delicious, and the tray of desserts looked very tempting.

The waitress with the dessert tray came over and asked if I was Tina. Confused, I replied yes. The waitress then set down an entire cake in front of me. I thought, *How sweet, my wonderful boyfriend had a cake made for me.* I then noticed that everyone in the restaurant was staring at me.

Finally, I looked at the cake more carefully. It read: "Tina, will you marry me?" I had to read it again, and then I jumped out of my seat and screamed "No, no, no" (people wondered if that was my answer).

Stunned, I walked backward into a corner and my husband-to-be (who was on bended knee with a ring in his outstretched hand) had to get up and follow me. I was finally able to compose myself enough to say yes, and I spent the entire evening staring at the beautiful ring on my finger.

—*Teneen M. Ardoin, East Rutherford, NJ*

SACRED HEART

*O*n our two-year anniversary of dating, I decided to take my girl-friend, Jennifer, to Paris to celebrate. I knew this would be a perfect place to propose to her, so I had to make all sorts of arrangements before our trip.

I picked out a beautiful diamond and had it placed in a tempo-rary setting (I wanted her to pick out the final setting to make sure it was exactly what she wanted). Then I asked Jennifer's parents for her hand in marriage and they happily gave me permission to marry their daughter. Now I only had one more thing to do—actually ask her!

A few weeks later, Jennifer and I were off to France. After a seven-hour snow delay, which caused us to spend the night in Detroit, we arrived in Paris. I didn't know exactly where I was going to propose, so I carried the ring with me at all times. I figured I would pop the question when the moment felt right. By the third day, I was getting a little nervous that the moment might never happen. It was St. Patrick's Day, our official anniversary, and we decided to begin the day with a hike up to the Sacré-Coeur, which is a cathedral at the highest point in Paris. When we arrived, we went inside, looked around, lit a candle, and said a prayer together. As we shared this spir-itual moment, something inside me began to stir.

We then ventured to the dome at the top of the cathedral. We walked up a dark, spiral staircase, with more than three hundred steps. When we finally reached the top, Jennifer was so excited by the beautiful view that she wanted to take some pictures. My heart started beating like crazy as I tried to figure out if this was the right place. I quickly decided that it was.

I ran around to the other side of the dome to take the ring out of my wallet and put it in the ring box. When I went back to Jennifer, she had already started back down the stairs, so I had to call her back up. Guiding her over to a place that had an amazing view of the city, I couldn't wait to express what I was feeling inside. I looked into her eyes and told her how much I loved her, how wonderful I thought she was, and how excited I got when I thought about spending the rest of my life with her. As she began to shake a bit, I sat down with her on a beautiful stone bench. I pulled the box out of my pocket, got down on one knee, and said, "Jennifer, I want to spend the rest of my life with you and I want you to be my wife. Will you marry me?" Jennifer started crying, hugged me, and said, "Are you serious?" I replied, "You have a ring in your hand, don't you?" Then she said, "I would love to." It was definitely the right moment.

—*Rich Berner, Manhattan Beach, CA*

GOING ONCE, GOING TWICE, SOLD

*O*ne Saturday in October our church was hosting a silent auction to benefit needy Denver children. It was to be held at the same hotel where my boyfriend, Byron, had asked me to be his girlfriend six months earlier. Though we had no money and were not planning on purchasing anything, we decided it would be fun to have a big night out together.

Once at the auction, Byron encouraged me to look around and to bid on anything I saw that I might want. I argued that we really could not afford to make any big purchases at that time. However, he had his eye on a laptop computer. He asked me to write my ticket number, 334, on the laptop. Of course, I refused.

Later that evening, as the auctioneer was closing the bidding, Byron insisted that we sit in front to see who won the bids. I remember thinking, "Why does it matter? We didn't bid on anything." We listened as the emcee announced the top bidders and awarded them their merchandise.

Finally, the emcee announced that there was one last item, which they did not have on display. They were offering a rain check to the top bidder, ticket number 334.

"That's my number, but I didn't bid on anything," I told Byron.

"Oh, I bid on some things for you," he replied.

"I hope it's not that computer. You know we can't afford it," I warned.

"Just go up there and see what it is," he said.

As I walked up to the podium, I was so upset over him spending this money that I didn't notice he had followed me up to the stage.

The emcee handed Byron the microphone and stepped back. I had no idea what was going on until I noticed the ring box in Byron's hand.

He got down on one knee and took my hand. Before he could say anything, I screamed and ran off the stage saying, "I can't do this here. Not now." My friends were backstage and they calmed me down and pushed me back onstage. Once I was back there, Byron knelt down, took my hand, and said, "Elycia, you and I have known each other for about a year and a half and have been dating for six months. I love you very much."

I was so embarrassed I couldn't look him in the eyes. People from the audience were yelling, "Look at him!" I answered back, "No, I can't," just as Byron asked me to be his wife. I looked down into his bewildered face and realized that he thought that had been my answer to his proposal. He took my hand, looked deep into my eyes, and asked me again. I looked straight into his gaze and said, "Of course."

—*Elycia Cook, Highlands Ranch, CO*

A BITING PROPOSAL

*M*y boyfriend and I went to Blimpie's, our favorite restaurant, for lunch. I ordered my usual to go—roast beef, cheese, lettuce, and tomatoes, with mayonnaise on both slices of bread. We took our food to my sister-in-law's house around the corner. I was so hungry that I barely had my coat off before I was biting the sandwich. I stopped abruptly, however, because I had bitten into something very hard. I lifted up the bread and there, lying on top of the lettuce, was an engagement ring. My very amused boyfriend then asked me to be his wife. I said, "Yes" and cried, not only because I was happy but also because my tooth was hurting. We've been married four years, and we still enjoy eating Blimpie's sandwiches for lunch.

—*Shirley Morales, Bronx, NY*

LOVE SEAT

J was a groomsman in a friend's wedding on the day that I proposed to my girlfriend. Early that morning, I went to the hotel where the reception was going to be held. After clearing my plan with the hotel's front desk manager (who started to cry upon hearing it), I set up our room in a way that would be both meaningful and memorable.

My friends helped me move a couch from my house into the hotel room—this was the same couch where my girlfriend and I had first kissed almost three years ago. Along with the couch, we adorned the room with dozens of roses and candles. I also chilled a bottle of champagne in anticipation of our celebration and wrapped up some bridal magazines to give to her after I proposed. The last essential item—the ring—rested in the petals of a silver rose on a night table next to the couch.

After my friend's wedding, I joined my girlfriend at the reception. Ironically, I caught the bride's garter that night. As the party was winding down, we went back to our room. She was very confused as to why the couch was there. The reason became clear, however, after I proposed to her and she said yes.

After I explained to her all of the preparations that went into this magical night and how I had asked her father's permission two weeks earlier, she was so excited that we returned to the reception to share our happiness with everyone who remained.

—*Francis T. Cermak, Downers Grove, IL*

THE BEST LAID PLANS

*E*ven though Amy and I had only been dating about ten months, I knew I wanted to spend the rest of my life with her. Now, all I had to do was plan a romantic, funny, intimate setting to pop the question.

I had picked out a simple one-carat, round diamond in a platinum setting with baguettes on the side (with the help of a few well-placed questions to Amy). I reserved a suite at the Waldorf Astoria hotel in New York City for Sunday, December 22, our one-year anniversary. All was going well until Amy found out about a terrific deal on a Caribbean cruise, which left on December 14 and arrived back on December 21. Talk about perfect timing: We can go away for a beautiful vacation, come back, get settled, and the next day, get engaged. What actually transpired was not-so-perfect.

About two weeks before the cruise, we found out that the ship was overbooked. We were bumped to another ship, which was going to the same places, but it left one day later and returned on our anniversary. I didn't panic and dealt with this change of plans. With a little help from the staff at the Waldorf, I arranged to lock the ring in one of the hotel's safety deposit boxes for the week that we would be on the cruise. I didn't want Amy to accidentally find the ring, and I also didn't want it to burn a hole in my pocket on the cruise and have a premature engagement.

Everything was set—the ring was locked in the hotel safe, my cousins would decorate our room at the Waldorf with "Happy Anniversary" banners, and I reserved a limousine to take us from the airport to the hotel.

Any guy who has gone through a proposal knows the hell I went through on the seven-day cruise. I believe I became physically ill one night just worrying if all of my plans would turn out OK.

The big day finally arrived. The ship docked at about 8:00 A.M. in Florida, and the passengers disembarked. By now, I could feel an uneasiness in my stomach, and I was trying desperately to put the evening's plans out of my mind. After all, it was only about 10:00 A.M., and our flight back to New York wasn't until 4:00 P.M. Fortunately, I had some relatives in Florida who could help us pass the time.

Before long, we were at a quaint little outdoor café with my relatives. One of my cousins had just ended an engagement on bad terms and decided to vent her frustrations to all of us. She went on and on about how she wasn't going to marry for love anymore, she was going to marry for money. In fact, she said that if the next guy didn't give her at least a two-carat ring, she wouldn't even consider the proposal. That was about all I could take. I lost it! I started screaming at her: "A ring is a symbol of love, not some material thing that gets examined for how much it's worth. It doesn't matter how big the ring is, it's the thought behind it!" My face turned red and Amy rubbed my shoulders to calm me down. She asked the obvious question: "What's wrong with you?" I squeamishly apologized and quickly changed the subject.

Finally, it was time to go home. We arrived at the airport and found out that our flight would be delayed for one to two hours due to a mechanical difficulty. Great, just what I needed—more delays. The hour and a half felt like one hundred years. The plane got stuck on the runway for an additional half-hour and hit plenty of turbulence on the way home.

We finally landed at Newark Airport and our bags took an eternity to arrive. We grabbed them and headed to our waiting limousine. Amy asked me about the limousine, and I told her that I thought it would be nice to take it home in honor of our one-year anniversary.

When we pulled into the drop-off area of the Waldorf Astoria, Amy still wanted to know what was happening. I told her that I thought it would be nice to spend the night at a posh hotel in honor of our one-year anniversary. She agreed.

We walked to the reception desk and got the key to our room. I asked Amy to wait for me for one minute because I had to use the bathroom. She didn't understand why I couldn't just wait until we went to our room. I then went to the safety deposit box, grabbed the ring, and joined Amy.

We opened the door to our room. It was decorated with many beautiful "Happy Anniversary" banners and gorgeous flower arrangements. I couldn't wait. I still had my jacket on and was pulling four sets of bags from the trip. I dropped the bags, grabbed Amy by the hand, pushed her down on the couch, and dropped down on both knees. I pulled out the ring and said, "Amy, I love you very much, and I want to spend the rest of my life with you. Will you marry me?" She immediately began to cry and sputtered over and over again, "I can't believe you did this." Finally, by the fourth or fifth "I can't believe you did this," I said, "I'd really like an answer now, whether it be yes or no." Amy said yes, and the deed was done.

—*Steve Gold, New York, NY*

HOPELESSLY DEVOTED

$\mathcal{I}$ met my girlfriend, Kim, at work. It was her first day, and my boss was taking her around introducing her to everyone. Before we had spoken one word, I felt something come over me. Something extremely powerful that I can't explain other than to say that I knew she was the one for me. When my boss finally got to my cube and introduced us, I was speechless.

Over the next few days I agonized about how I was going to ask her out on a date, but she beat me to the punch. We went out that Friday and have been together ever since. A little more than two months after we met, Kim wanted to see *Grease* on Broadway. I bought tickets to the matinee show. My plan was starting to take shape. I called a family friend who worked at the Jewelry Exchange in Manhattan and made an appointment to see him about the ring two weeks before the show.

I had made reservations at the Doral Park Hotel on Park Avenue for our weekend stay. Dinner reservations were set at a restaurant called Sam's on 47th Street. Everything was going according to plan.

When we arrived at the theater, we took our seats in the fourth row of the orchestra section. Before the show, the actor who plays Vince Fountaine does something they call a Sock Hop—a little audience participation and fun time before the show starts. I passed a note to an usher to give to Vince. She passed it along to him, and when he read it, I saw Vince smile.

About ten minutes later, Vince said, "Everyone please quiet down and direct your attention to the stage. I need everyone's complete attention." The entire theater, about one thousand people, fell silent and stared at Vince up on the stage.

Next, Vince asked, "Is there a Kim Oliver in the house? Kim Oliver, are you here?" Of course, Kim was there and she is definitely not the type of person who likes to be a public spectacle, but she raised her hand. Vince called her onstage. She went up, they talked for a few minutes, and then he asked her, "Are you here with anyone?"

Kim said that she was there with her boyfriend, Greg—me. Vince invited me to join them onstage. He and I talked for a few minutes, and then he said to me, "Greg, I understand there is something that you want to ask Kim."

I replied, "As a matter of fact, yes, there is." He handed me the microphone. I got down on one knee and proposed to Kim onstage at the Eugene O'Neill Theatre in front of all 1,000 audience members. She started to cry and said yes through her tears. You couldn't really understand what she said, so Vince asked her to repeat it, for fun.

The actress who played Sandy came running out from backstage, half made up, in curlers, and asked, "Can I see the ring?" The rest of the cast followed and we hung out with them onstage for a little while before we returned to our seats for the show to begin. I still don't think Kim actually remembers watching the show, because all she did was look at the ring the entire time.

—*Greg Gibel, Royersford, PA*

ROLE REVERSAL

$\mathcal{F}$or months, Frank and I had discussed marriage. One of his comments struck me: Not wanting to adhere to tradition, he said that he would never get down on one knee and ask me to marry him. I knew he was the man I wanted to marry, so I decided to do the proposing myself!

It would be marriage number three for both of us, so I wanted to make the proposal something we'd never forget. I went to many jewelers and asked if they carried engagement rings for men. I finally had a ring custom-made. I decided to propose on Frank's birthday, February 4, at a jazz club we frequented. It wasn't unusual for our group of friends to celebrate birthdays and anniversaries in this manner, so he wasn't suspicious when I suggested we go.

On the night of his birthday, we all met at Frank's place and headed off to the club. I was a bit nervous, but very excited and couldn't wait to see the look of shock on his face when I proposed. After the band played several songs, the emcee announced that it was Frank's birthday and asked him to come forward. Frank was puzzled, but he went up anyway. As he stood there, center stage, I took a deep breath and walked over to him. I then got down on one knee and asked Frank to marry me. He looked so surprised! As he said yes, I placed the ring on his finger. He looked at me with tears in his eyes and said, "I love you," as our friends gathered around to see his engagement ring. It was definitely a moment neither one of us will ever forget. We were married three years later.

—*Dale T. McCants, Cranbury, NJ*

SHE'S AN ANGEL

$\mathcal{G}$reg and I had been dating for more than seven years and living together for one. To be honest, I had all but given up on him ever proposing to me. Around Christmas of our seventh year together, Greg asked me what gift I wanted. I made up something on the spot, even though my true desire was an engagement ring.

I have a very bad habit: If I find a gift under the Christmas tree with my name on it, I shake it very hard to try to guess its contents. Needless to say, I wasn't very surprised when Greg waited until Christmas Eve to put my gift under the tree. But when he went to sleep that night, I shook the box. It sounded like a puzzle! I went to sleep disappointed, knowing that there was no ring in that box.

I awoke early on Christmas morning and immediately called my parents who live six hundred miles away. We opened our gifts over the phone and ended our conversation by wishing each other a very Merry Christmas. I then waited impatiently for Greg to get up. When he did, I had him open his gifts first. Then it was my turn. I opened my present only to find a box of dominoes that looked like they were about twenty years old. It was all I could do to not show my utter dismay. However, inside the box I discovered a card. It read, "Your real gift is on our tree! Good Luck! Love, Greg."

I began to search the tree. After what seemed like an eternity (actually five minutes), I found my real Christmas present. Sitting in the hands of the angel on top of our tree was a ring. I immediately recognized it because it was a family heirloom. I took the ring from the angel, and then Greg took it from me. I sat on the couch, and Greg got down on one knee in front of me. As tears rolled down my face, Greg proposed. I could not stop crying as I hugged and kissed him and said yes. No Christmas will ever mean more to me.

On a side note, the ring belonged to Greg's mother's godmother, Claire. She and her husband never had any children of their own. Therefore, Claire always treated Greg's mother like a daughter, and Greg and his sister like they were her grandchildren. She had given the ring to Greg a few years earlier to use when he was ready.

—*Melanie Cobb, Fresno, CA*

THE SOUND OF MUSIC

*I*t was the evening of the release party for my new album. After finishing my singing performance, I waited in the wings to watch my boyfriend, Orrin, perform some of his jazz tunes for the crowd. He began playing one of his more popular original tunes and suddenly stopped. He took the microphone and asked me to come onstage. I was a bit confused, but I walked over to him. He asked me to stand center stage, right next to the piano. He then sat down and began to play a new song he had written for me called, "Dawn Marie." He sang.

I never thought that we
Would spend eternity
In each other's arms

Now nothing seems as right
I just want you in my arms now

Please don't let go
I don't know
What I would do
Without you Dawn Marie

Now, there are two little boys
Depending on our love
And everlasting joy

Let's start our family
Will you marry me
Dawn Marie?

I want you
In my life
Forever until the end
My best friend

I totally lost it and I began sobbing so hysterically that I couldn't even speak. Orrin stood up from the piano and got down on one knee. The bass player handed him the ring and Orrin placed it on my finger. We just kissed and embraced each other, and for that instant, I forgot where I was and that there were one hundred people eagerly awaiting my answer. At this point, the drummer took the microphone and said, "We all heard the question, so what's your answer?" I grabbed the microphone, still sobbing uncontrollably, and said, "Oh my goodness, I love this man so much. Of course I'll marry him!"

—*Dawn Warren, Philadelphia, PA*

THERE'S NO PLACE LIKE HOME

*M*y boyfriend and I both recently graduated from Columbia University with master's degrees. Because student housing was no longer an option, we decided to bite the bullet and cohabitate. Being something of an old-fashioned gal, I was secretly worried about living with a man before marriage. One day in May, we found ourselves looking for an apartment in an industrial neighborhood in an outer borough of New York City.

After a long day of apartment hunting, we decided we had earned a nice dinner. We went to a seedy hamburger joint and ordered two deluxe cheeseburgers. The place was a real dive but somehow comforting in the way that seedy diners can sometimes be. For some reason or another, I made a rueful remark about how we were about to "live in sin" once we had secured an apartment. My boyfriend paused for only a moment before he said:

"Well, that doesn't have to be the case."

Bewildered, I replied, "What do you mean that doesn't have to be the case?"

"Well," he said, "we could get married."

"Sure," I said, "someday."

"Why someday?" he asked. "Why not sooner than that?"

I put my cheeseburger down on my plate and looked at him apprehensively. "What are you saying?"

With a smile of satisfaction mixed with bashfulness, my boyfriend said, "I am asking you to marry me."

"No way!" I exploded.

"Yes, way!"

"You're kidding, right? You're not serious."

"If you don't believe me, call your mother," he said. "I asked her for permission for your hand more than a month ago."

Boy, did this drive the point home. I was so stunned that I had to excuse myself. I went outside and smoked three cigarettes in a row while my boyfriend watched me from the table, laughing. Once I had recovered, I returned to the table and promptly said yes.

We saved the menus from that little diner where he proposed, and my fiancé asked for permission to take some plastic flowers from the table vase as a memento. Occasionally, we still drive past that diner—which is only a few blocks from the place where we eventually moved in together. We moved into an apartment located on Bliss Street—an apt name, wouldn't you say?

—*Jan Watson Collins, Woodside, NY*

THAT'S AMORE!

$\mathcal{M}$y fiancé, William, and I met seven years ago when we were seniors in college and have dated exclusively since then. Last spring for my birthday, he told me that he was taking me on a surprise trip for spring break. (I teach high school English.) He requested that I pack for a climate of fifty to seventy degrees. I guessed that we were going to San Francisco because it's close by, or possibly New York because William's cousin lives there.

On the day of our trip, William made me wear a blindfold on our drive to the airport and through the terminal. When we arrived at the gate, he took off the blindfold. I was shocked—we were at the Alitalia gate boarding a flight for Venice, Italy. I screamed, jumped up and down, and thanked William profusely.

In Venice, we had a room on the canal in a centuries-old building. The next day we went to the Murano glass factory and had lunch in St. Mark's Square. It was drizzling, but that didn't dampen our spirits. It surprised me, though, when William suggested a gondola ride in the rain. He hired an Italian singer to serenade us and a musician to play the accordion while we took our moist gondola ride. About halfway through our trip—in front of Mozart's home—William proposed to me.

The music was playing, the love of my life was with me, and we were in Venice, a city that is synonymous with love. How could I not say yes? As we passed under each bridge, William yelled, "I'm getting married" and "she said yes." Bystanders clapped and cheered. It was the most surreal, romantic, and exciting event of my life.

—*Jane Ojanpera, Redondo Beach, CA*

AN ENGAGEMENT TO REMEMBER

$\mathcal{M}$y first date with Samantha was a blind date. That evening, we talked for hours. We discovered that we had a lot in common, including an affinity for movies. We spoke about some of our favorite films, both critically acclaimed classics and those that had shaped our lives and influenced our thinking (like the fact that *St. Elmo's Fire* influenced my desire to attend Georgetown University, my alma mater). We discovered that we both loved the 1994 Warren Beatty and Annette Bening movie *Love Affair,* a remake of the Cary Grant classic, *An Affair to Remember.*

During a whirlwind romance of six weeks, unlike any that either of us had ever experienced, Sam and I found ourselves on an Amtrak train from Philadelphia to Connecticut. We were going to stay with her family following her sister's wedding that weekend. Knowing that she was the woman I wanted to spend the rest of my life with, I had just picked up an engagement ring and was waiting for the right moment to propose. I didn't have an exact plan, but I knew my proposal should incorporate our mutual love of movies.

At my suggestion, we disembarked in New York City so we could catch the Sunday matinee of *The Lion King* on Broadway. Unfortunately, the show was sold out and we were unable to get tickets. We decided to stay in Manhattan overnight anyway. Within an hour, we had checked into the Essex House (a central backdrop in *Love Affair*) and I had purchased tickets to another show. I also made late reservations at one of the hottest restaurants in New York. We wanted a snack, so Samantha picked up the most wonderful picnic lunch, which we enjoyed right in the middle of Central Park.

While we ate, we started talking seriously about our relationship and our future together. Things were falling right into place.

As we walked back to the Essex House, Samantha said that we should take a nap before leaving for the theater and dinner. I told her to go ahead; I'd be right up. When she was out of sight, I put my plan into action. Earlier, I had purchased a beautiful postcard of the Empire State Building, upon which I had written:

Samantha—
If you are 100 percent positive that you wish to spend the rest of your life with Michael J. Burwick, please report to the lobby promptly at 4:30 p.m. and ask for Hector.
Love, Michael.

As most movie fans know, the Empire State Building is where the lovers in *An Affair the Remember* and *Love Affair* were supposed to meet and to pledge their love. I made arrangements with Hector, one of the Essex House doormen, to have a limousine ready at the appropriate time and asked him to inform the driver of my plan. He was under strict orders not to answer any questions from Samantha. The concierge had the postcard delivered to our room immediately.

Meanwhile, I set off for the Empire State Building. I explained my plan to one of the security chiefs and enlisted his help. I was ushered past the lines of waiting tourists into one of the elevators to the observation deck and I began my wait.

Not long after I arrived I saw Samantha emerge from an elevator. The sun was setting over Manhattan. Through the crowd of tourists, our eyes met and we smiled knowingly at each other. We made our way toward each other and attempted to find a quiet spot. It was tough, but we managed to locate a break in the crowd. I started to get down on one knee, but Sam quite forcefully told me, "Stop." My heart sank because I thought she was rejecting my proposal. But she quickly explained that the ground was filthy and she didn't want me to soil my suit. I shrugged and put my knee back down, and asked if Samantha would, indeed, honor me by agreeing to marry me. Upon hearing her reply, "Definitely!" I placed the engagement ring on her finger.

We left and took a taxi to an upscale bar where we toasted our engagement with champagne and spoke to our parents on the phone. To cap the evening off, we saw a terrific off-Broadway show and dined at a fantastic restaurant. I couldn't have asked for a more perfect night or a more perfect woman to start a future with.

—*Michael J. Burwick, Miami, FL*

KEEP ON TRUCKIN'

J had finally made the decision to move from New York to Chicago to be with my boyfriend, Clif. I left my job, packed my boxes, and rented a Penske truck for the long drive. Clif and I loaded up all my belongings and hit the road. I knew it was the right decision for the future of our relationship, but I never imagined I would get engaged along the way.

We had been driving all night, and at about 6:30 A.M., he started telling me some deep story about us traveling this road together to be united, yada, yada, yada. But I wasn't hearing him, because we had already been on the road for fourteen hours and I just wanted to get to his apartment and get to sleep.

I was blunt with him. "It's not like you have a ring or something," I said. I didn't think he would propose right then at that hour of the morning while we were driving on the Interstate with me feeling very gross about my stale breath. He looked at me and said, "What if I do have a ring and what if I'm asking you right now?" Then he pulled the ring out of his pocket and asked me to marry him. After I picked my face off the floor of the truck, I said, "Yes."

I'm glad he did it then because he caught me totally off guard. It was the last place I would have ever suspected to get a proposal. Now whenever we see a Penske truck, we smile at each other.

—*Shawne Steele, Chicago, IL*

ALL IN A DAY'S WORK

I had no doubts that Michelle was meant to be my wife. So, I figured it this way . . . acquire the ring in mid-September and then pop the question some two months later, around the time of our one-year anniversary in late November. What a plan!

We both live in San Diego and I was scheduled to go on a business trip to Pennsylvania for two days. Before I left, I contacted my father and stepmother in Pittsburgh and asked them to help me get the ring. Michelle wanted an oval-style diamond, which are hard to find. Finally, after many phone calls, we found one in New York and had it flown into Pittsburgh, where I had it mounted. The ring was finished on the last day of my trip, so I had it sent overnight express to San Diego.

There I was on a Friday morning with this ring. Forget waiting until November to pop the question. I was supposed to meet Michelle for lunch at 11:00 A.M. But before that, I had to track down her mom. I found her at work and asked her permission to ask her daughter to marry me. She immediately burst into tears and exclaimed, "Yes, Rob, go, go, go!" I thanked her and took off to meet Michelle for lunch.

On the way to Michelle's office, I stopped and picked up a single rose. I had sent her a dozen roses two days prior and one had died that morning. This one was to replace it. I got out of my car, ring in my pocket, rose in my hand, heart pounding through my chest, and walked to the entrance of her office building. She works in a large, wide-open office area with many coworkers. I opened the door and walked straight toward her, trying to keep my eyes focused on her and not the coworkers in the area.

She greeted me with the usual hug. I returned the hug, backed away just a bit, placed my forehead on hers, and whispered, "I just can't wait, honey." She, of course, had no idea what I was talking about. I gently sat her down in her chair, get down on one knee, and reached into my pocket for the ring.

"What are you doing?" she uttered. A nearby coworker, who had been watching the whole scene, exclaimed in a loud voice for all to hear, "What the hell do you *think* he's doing?" I pulled the ring box from my pocket, opened it, and asked Michelle to be my wife. She immediately started crying. After she said "yes," we hugged for what seemed to be the most uplifting moment of my entire life! Her coworkers immediately rallied around for congratulations and hugs.

—*Rob and Michelle Aarnes, San Diego, CA*

A GOOD SIGN

J was running late for work and wasn't paying much attention to anything except the clock. I hurriedly parked my car and rushed inside. I immediately began working, worried about being so late.

I glanced up and noticed my boss walking toward my desk. I was afraid he was coming over to chastise me. He stopped by the window and asked me to come over and look at something. As I joined him, I looked out the window and noticed there was a new billboard across the street. It read, "Shawn, will you marry me? Love, Eric."

As you can imagine, I was shocked. I had to read it several times before it registered in my mind exactly what the sign said. I ran to my desk and made several attempts to contact Eric by phone.

Just as I was calming down, I looked up and there was Eric with a photographer and videographer in tow. He made a beautiful, spiritual speech to me in front of all of my coworkers. Then he knelt down on one knee, presented a lovely diamond ring to me, and proposed again.

My heart was beating a mile a minute. I was shaking and crying, but of course my answer was "yes." I believe that if my answer had been anything else, one of my excited and tearful coworkers would have said yes for me.

—*Shawn N. Doman, Missouri City, TX*

KEY TO MY HEART

*O*n a Friday in December, I took my girlfriend, Kerrie, to CJ's Pub (a local bar) for a burger. My intention was to make it seem like any other night to her. Near the end of our meal, I became very serious and told her I had something very important I wanted to discuss with her. I pulled out an envelope addressed to her that looked like a love note. As I took it out of my pocket, I stated that I had found the letter outside of our apartment door and she had some explaining to do. Needless to say, she was puzzled.

When she opened the letter, she found a note with a key taped to the bottom of the page. The message was spelled out in letters cut out from a magazine. It read, "Where does this key belong?" At this point, she knew it was a ruse, but she seemed pleasantly amused. With a big smile on my face I asked where she thought the key was from. After a few guesses, I had to give her a hint by asking her, "Where have you always wanted to stay?"

She had always been enamored with a bed and breakfast in our town called Beiger Mansion. When she guessed the place, I suggested we go there and find out. As we were driving there, she repeatedly said that she did not want to waste our time if that was not the place. I drove on.

When we reached the mansion, I prodded her to go to the front desk to ask if the key she possessed belonged there. When she asked the man behind the counter, she was given a rose with a note that stated, "Welcome to Beiger Mansion. Go up and sit on the bed."

We went up to the room. It was perfect. The furniture was authentic early 1900s style, complete with a clawfoot tub in the bathroom. I was impressed to find that the innkeeper kept his promise to have a cold bottle of champagne chilling in an ice bucket in the corner of the room. Feeling a bit nervous about the unfolding events, I watched in silence as Kerrie began her adventure.

Kerrie went to the bed as the note had instructed and there she found another note with a rose attached. The note was a romantic poem that directed her to another part of the room. She went to that spot and found another note with a rose attached.

This scavenger hunt continued. On the eleventh note, there was a rose and a romantic saying leading her to another spot in the room. When she went to the final hiding place, which was the pillow on the bed, I was sure to place myself directly behind her. I watched with anticipation as she reached behind the pillow to find a note and a rose, which gave her a perfect dozen. On this note I had written, "Will you marry me?" When she turned to face me with tears in her eyes, I had the ring in hand and asked her myself, "Will you marry me?" Thank God she answered yes!

One last note: My wife swears that I have not been romantic since that day, which was more than two and a half years ago. I keep telling her that when someone takes that much time and energy to be that romantic, it takes at least a decade to recharge.

—*Luke and Kerrie Conway, Mishawaka, IN*

PICTURE PERFECT

$\mathcal{M}$y boyfriend, Jeff, and I had been to Vail, Colorado, in 1992 for a skiing vacation and returned in 1993 for another one. The first year, we had a professional photographer take our picture on the top of the mountain, and Jeff suggested we take one again the second time. He had asked me to take the picture on the first day of the trip, but it was snowing and I didn't feel like taking the picture with my hair all wet. I was oblivious to how this messed up his plans. So, on the second day, I agreed to take the picture before the first ski run of the day.

Once we reached the summit, Jeff skied ahead of me and got the photographer's attention. We took a bunch of pictures, and for the last one the photographer asked me to get down in the snow in the "bunny" position (I was lying down with my skis crossed behind my head and Jeff was standing above me). I hoped the pictures turned out well, as they would be a fun reminder of the great trip we were having.

We skied for the rest of the day and when we were done, we went down to the "Sharp Shooter" gallery in Vail Village to look at the proofs of our pictures. Little did I know that the whole gallery was in on Jeff's secret and that the photographer was waiting for us.

He showed us all of our pictures on a huge screen and the final one was the "bunny" pose. However, the photographer zoomed in on a shirt with the words, "Mara, will you marry me?" printed on it. I thought it was some kind of joke that the photographer was playing on us. But then he zoomed out and I saw the whole picture. There Jeff was, standing on the top of Vail Mountain with a huge smile, wearing the shirt for everyone to see with me lying below him, totally oblivious to his actions and simply thinking how cute the picture would be.

When I looked next to me, Jeff was down on one knee with a velvet blue ring box in hand. He popped the question with the entire gallery watching and clapping. I was in complete shock because, although we had dated for nearly six years, I was only twenty-one years old. I immediately started crying when someone asked, "So what did she say?" I said, "Yes!" We had the most amazing wedding and have been happily married for almost four years.

—Mara Kaplan-Kaliner, Media, PA

ALL IN THE FAMILY

$\mathcal{B}$rian and I became engaged at the wedding of my sister to his brother. At the reception, my sister informed all of the single women that when she threw the bouquet I should be the one to catch it. I should have suspected something, because when we gathered for the bouquet toss, my sister didn't exactly lob it—she bee-lined it directly to me. But I was just happy to have caught the lovely bouquet. For the garter toss, it was much the same. All of the guys were told to let Brian catch the garter, which of course he did.

After the respective tosses, Brian and I went out on the dance floor. He put the garter on me, and then the bandleader handed him the microphone. I thought, *What in the world is he going to say?* You customarily don't say anything during this sort of thing. Before I had a chance to guess, he placed the most beautiful diamond ring on my finger and asked me to marry him. The entire reception hall exploded in cheers.

I was caught so off guard that I didn't have an immediate reaction. My head was just spinning as our families swarmed around us for hugs, kisses, and pictures. I whispered urgently to Brian, "I need to go outside with you right now." It was difficult, but we finally made our way to the door.

Once outside, he looked at me and said, "Are we out here so you can say no?" I grabbed him, hugged and kissed him, and told him that my answer was, "Yes, yes, yes, and by the way, yes." All I wanted was a private moment in order to catch my breath and tell him how much I loved him.

As we sat in the moonlight holding hands, I realized I was not only the luckiest, but also the happiest girl on earth. I always knew that Brian was romantic, but he simply outdid himself with this proposal.

As the guests were leaving that night, they not only wished the bride and groom good luck, they also wished Brian and I happy planning.

We booked the same reception hall for one year later.

—*Jacqueline Weingart, Metuchen, NJ*

AMEN!

$\mathcal{E}$very Sunday I attend worship services at Hill Street Baptist Church in Roanoke, Virginia. My boyfriend, Reverend Johnny R. Stone, serves as pastor there. One Sunday, just before the benediction, Johnny announced that there was something he must do before he closed the service.

He began to talk about how he considered everyone in the congregation family, and he wanted them to be a part of something that was about to take place in his life. He said that by now, everyone knew there was someone very special in his life, and he wanted them to share in a very special event.

My heart skipped a beat. The entire congregation let out a loud gasp and then fell silent. Johnny invited me to join him in front of the altar. He descended from the pulpit while reciting 1st, Corinthians, verse 13. When he finished reading, he turned to face me. He looked deep into my tear-filled eyes and pledged his love, along with his heart and soul.

He then got down on both knees and presented me with the most gorgeous ring (which he had picked out himself) and asked me if I would marry him. Of course, I said yes. In fact, I was so nervous, shocked, happy, and overjoyed that my "yes" was barely audible. So, while still on his knees, Johnny yelled, "She said yes, y'all!" The church went wild.

—*Nina C. Stone, Roanoke, VA*

ALOHA

$\mathcal{R}$ob and I met in June 1996. He worked at the help desk at Quark, Inc., and I had just started a new job there. He invited me to go out with him on a few occasions, but I never said yes because I had heard that he was a huge flirt. I figured that he was just hitting on me, and besides, I didn't want to date someone from work.

But then, in November, our company announced its annual Quark Ski Trip. Rob and I were the trip coordinators and, during the planning of it, we got to know each other better. That's when I realized that he was someone I wanted to spend more time with.

A week after the trip, I called Rob. We went out to dinner. I don't remember what we ate, but I do remember thinking that he was a very captivating person. After that night, we were practically inseparable.

We went to Hawaii over Labor Day weekend, 1997. It was our first vacation alone. I had no expectations other than to spend quality time with Rob. It was a wonderful trip—sun, fun, and the man I loved. Who could ask for more? On our last night there, we went to Waimea Beach. No one was around, it was extremely dark, and all we could see was each other and the countless stars.

The waves were crashing on the shore, and the breeze was warm and mild. Rob sat behind me in the sand with his legs on either side of me. I leaned up against his chest, and we held each other. We talked about the stars and our beautiful vacation. Then Rob started to get very romantic.

He was building up the conversation by saying how much he cared for me and that he didn't know what he'd do without me.

Then he said, "I want you to marry me." I thought to myself, *Wow, that sounds so nice. It's so good to know that he feels that way.* I didn't say anything, because I thought he was talking about marriage as an idea—way off in the future.

Nothing prepared me for what Rob did next. He reached around with a lovely engagement ring on his pinkie. I was shocked, and I whimpered for a really long time. He finally had to ask me, "Is that a maybe?" I said, "No, that's an absolutely yes!" Before we left the beach, I grabbed a handful of sand to keep as a memento. It was perfect.

—*Mollie Rusher, Denver, CO*

ONLY IN AFRICA

$\mathcal{F}$or our seven-year anniversary, my boyfriend surprised me with a vacation to Morocco, Africa. We are both workaholics and had never taken a vacation together. I was psyched! He had already paid for and planned all of the travel arrangements, so all I had to do was pack.

We flew into Casablanca and spent three days there. Then we moved on to Marrakech. On our second day there, we toured the casbahs (markets), then we went to the pool for a couple of hours, swimming and lounging in the sun. After awhile, he went up to the room to get ready for a night out on the town. I soon followed. He finished getting ready before I did and went down to the lobby to wait for me.

I went down the big, marble, spiral staircase and he whisked me into a waiting Mercedes that took us to a Moroccan restaurant just outside the market square. We were ushered through the doorway and down some marble stairs that were covered with a red carpet. When we reached the bottom of the stairs, we were once again outside, in a beautiful courtyard. In the center were four smaller tables and two musicians—one playing a drum and the other a mandolin.

We were seated in the center of the courtyard under an orange-blossom tree. The sky was clear that night and the stars were shining through the leaves of the trees. We had a delicious dinner of couscous, chicken, and fresh veggies, topped off with some honeycakes and mint tea.

I held my glass of tea, thinking how perfect the night was, when he took my other hand in his. He was looking a little silly and, having known him for a long time, I started to think that something big was coming. As soon as he got down on one knee, I knew what he was about to do and looked around to see if anyone was watching (I think that secretly I wanted witnesses).

He told me how much he loved me and then asked me to be his wife. I didn't hesitate a second. I said, "Yes." It was then that I realized I was still holding my glass of tea with my other hand.

—*Koren Isherwood, Portland, ME*

SAY A LITTLE PRAYER

I met my future husband, John, when I was thirty-two. My younger brother, Steve, was playing basketball for Chapman College in Orange County, California and John was his coach. Steve was always telling both of us that we should meet because we would really get along. I finally made plans to fly down there one weekend, but chickened out at the last minute. I suggested that John come up to San Francisco, where I live, to coach at the week-long basketball camp for kids that my family put on every year.

John agreed, and a few weeks later we finally met at the camp. I thought he was a really great guy, but I didn't think he was interested in me at all. When the camp ended, I offered to drive him to the airport. His flight was delayed an hour, which gave us time to talk and really get to know each other. As he got on the plane, I remember thinking that I really liked him, but it was too bad that he lived so far away.

At 3:00 A.M. that night, my phone rang. It was John letting me know that he made it home safely and that he was looking forward to spending more time with me. I was a little shocked, but very happy about it. The next day, he sent me flowers. That was the start of a two-year long-distance relationship.

After a year of letters, many short visits, and huge phone bills, he took a job in Fresno as the head basketball coach at a small Christian college, which was only an hour away from me by car. Things were going well, and around Easter we began talking about marriage. Unfortunately, he was in no rush to do anything about it and I wasn't too sure that he was ever going to propose. So we broke up, but we did talk several times over the next few months. After a lot of serious discussions, I agreed to start seeing him again. In my mind, I was going to give him six months to take things to the next level, or I would know it was not meant to be.

Those six months passed and Easter arrived again. We spent that Sunday with my family having a nice brunch and then enjoying the afternoon by a lake reading chapters of a book to each other. Suddenly, John decided it was time to take me home. I didn't understand his rush, but he raced us back to my house, gathered his things together in a hurry, and jumped back into his car ready to return to Fresno. I was getting irritated at his odd behavior. I began to think that this was going to be the last time that I ever saw him, which upset me even more. He got out of the car and tried to calm me down. I wanted to be alone, but John insisted on trying to explain himself.

Finally, he blurted out, "Stop it or you'll ruin the surprise." I thought he was making that up to get me to stop talking, so I questioned him. He wouldn't tell me. I was frustrated and wanted to go back inside the house, but when I tried to open the front door, I realized that I had accidentally locked us out of my house. That's when I fell silent.

John looked at me and calmly said, "You want to know what the surprise was? Well, I'll tell you. I was planning on pretending to drive away and then coming back to tell you that I forgot my sunglasses by the lake. Then I was going to ask you to go with me to get them. When we got to the lake, I was going to take you to the water's edge and give you a special Bible. In the front, I had written a special inscription to you, and in the scriptures inside I had circled the words *will, you, marry,* and *me.* It was how I was going to propose to you." At that moment, I started to cry. I realized that I had just ruined the moment I had been waiting for my entire life.

Still a bit unsure if he was telling me the truth, I asked him to drive me to the lake. He did, and the sunglasses were right where he said they'd be. As I sat in the car still crying, he got out, retrieved the sunglasses, picked a yellow wild daisy, and sat down next to me. He handed me the flower and said, "Will you marry me?" I sniffled and said, "Only if you propose to me the way you wanted to." He took the Bible from the back seat, handed it to me, showed me the words he had circled, and asked me to marry him—again. I said, "Yes," and wondered how I could've ever doubted him.

Ten years and two children later, I still laugh at how crazy I was acting that day. And every time I go to church, I use that Bible. When I look at those four very special circled words, I smile.

—*Anonymous*

THE ROYAL TREATMENT

*O*n Halloween, my boyfriend, Chuck, and I decided to throw a party. I dressed as Jeannie from *I Dream of Jeannie*. He showed up as the Grim Reaper, which I thought was very cheesy. Regardless, I was having a great time with all of my friends, as well as both sets of our parents. Around 9:00 P.M., the phone rang. Chuck took the call and told me that it was two of our friends. He said that he was going to go outside and scare them.

Chuck left, and twenty minutes later his sister-in-law said to me, "There's a horse and carriage outside." I looked outside and saw a woman and a few kids getting out of the carriage. Suddenly, a horn sounded and one of the kids ran up to the door and yelled, "The king is here! The king is here!"

Everyone at the party headed outside. As we all stood wondering what was going on, Chuck's best friend pulled out a video camera. That's when I saw Chuck sitting in the carriage dressed in an elaborate king's outfit, complete with a velvet robe, tunic, black tights, and a crown. We all formed a semi-circle around the carriage to see what was going to happen next.

Some of our friends were dressed as knights, a princess, squires, and a dragon. Chuck stood up and began "knighting" each of his friends. He then stepped out of the carriage and announced that he was looking for his "queen."

He stopped in front of me, dropped to one knee, and handed me a crown. He then presented me with a velvet rose resting on a white satin pillow and asked me to open the petals of the rose. As I did, he said, "I would like you to be my bride."

I couldn't believe what was happening. Everyone started screaming and I began to shake from all the excitement. As I opened the rose, I saw the most beautiful ring I could have ever imagined. Chuck looked at me and asked for my answer. I said, "Yes!" and gave him a big hug and kiss.

Chuck took my hand and led me to the carriage. We stepped inside, snuggled under some blankets, and rode off into the night.

—*Priscilla Scarano, Coppell, TX*

OH, WHAT A NIGHT

*O*n Valentine's Day, exactly one year after our first date, my boyfriend, Tim, planned an evening out for us in Westwood, California. When I arrived at my apartment, where Tim was supposed to meet me, instead of my beau I found a bouquet of ten red roses. Along with the roses was a loving card with instructions that I must engage in a scavenger hunt in order to complete the dozen.

My first destination was to be the site of our first dinner together. Once there, I was to go to the bar and order my favorite drink. I went to the Westwood Brewing Company and ordered a drink. The bartender returned with a huge smile, a red rose, and a note sending me to the theater where we had caught a movie on our first date.

Clutching my eleven roses, I trekked to the theater on Gayley Avenue where we had seen *Bed of Roses* the year before. The ticket taker was happy to present me with another rose directing me to the site of our first goodnight kiss, the steps of my Delta Delta Delta sorority house.

I must have been a sight that afternoon, walking through the streets of Westwood in a black dress and heels, carrying a dozen roses, and wearing a huge smile. I could not decide whether to attribute my rush of adrenaline to the mile I must have walked by then, or the mounting suspicion I had that this was not going to be just another Valentine's Day.

By the time I turned the corner and saw my future husband leaning nonchalantly on the porch of my house, my emotions produced a rush of joyful tears. As I reached the top step, he fell to one knee and, professing his love for me, asked me to be his wife. I wholeheartedly accepted!

He presented me with a diamond ring, which he had chosen himself—the exact ring I would have picked out had I done the shopping. Only after the cheers began from the upstairs window did I realize that our exchange had been caught on film by some of my sorority sisters. I later learned that Tim had spent the better part of a month letting all of our family and friends in on the plan. He had even asked for my parent's blessing on a trip we had taken to their home in northern California the month before! Tim is the most romantic husband a woman could ever hope for. He continues to make every day as special for me as that Valentine's Day so long ago.

—*Melissa DeCinces, Laguna Beach, CA*

CLOSE ENCOUNTERS

*B*uying Nadine's engagement ring was quite an adventure. Nadine's days off are usually Tuesday and Wednesday, when she often meets me for lunch. I planned to pick up the ring on Friday. As luck would have it, I found out late Thursday afternoon that Nadine was given Friday off. She had a few errands to run in the morning but wanted to meet me for lunch. I figured I wouldn't be able to get the ring at all. At about 12:30 P.M., however, when she still hadn't called, I figured something must have come up and I was in the clear to run my errand.

The jeweler's shop is about ten miles from my work, so I drove down there as fast as I could. I had just started talking to the jeweler when my pager went off—Nadine. I excused myself and went out to call her from my cell phone.

Her: "Where are you?"

Me: "I'm at lunch."

Her: "Where?"

Me: "Carl's Jr."

Her: "Oh, I just passed it. I'll turn around and join you." (Oh, no!)

Me: "Umm . . . I'm not there. I'm actually in North Park." (A very bad part of town.)

Her: "Why are you in North Park?"

Me: "Umm . . . I'm running an errand. Why don't you meet me at . . ." (I run to the curb to see what's around.) "McDonald's."

Her: "Okay."

She was about ten minutes away, which should give me just enough time to make my purchase. I ran back into the store and explained my situation to the jeweler. Ten minutes later, I was out the door. I ran to my car. It wouldn't start! Here I was, in the wrong part of town, with an expensive ring in my pocket and a car that won't start.

I ran across the street to McDonald's. Nadine pulled in right when I got to the driveway I had to duck behind some cars so she wouldn't see me. As she was parking, I casually strode up to her car.

Her: "Where's your car?"

Me: "It broke down. Let's eat."

When we finished our lunch, I told her I needed to make a phone call. I didn't have time to get my car fixed and didn't want it to get towed. I ran to the curb to call the jeweler from my cell phone but I couldn't get a signal. I ran back to McDonald's where they told me that the closest phone booth was across the street.

I told Nadine I was heading over to the phone booth, but instead ran to the jeweler. When I walked into the shop, all out of breath, everyone stared at me like I was an alien from outer space. Of course, with my luck, the lady who had helped me earlier was with a customer. I waited patiently. When she was finished, I explained to her about my car. She told me not to worry.

Nadine took me back to work and I finished up my workday. After work, I got a ride back to my car. Just for the hell of it, I thought I would try to start it one more time. Sure enough, it started on the first turn. It seems that when I had tried to start it earlier, I was so nervous that I forgot to turn off the alarm and the ignition-kill function stopped me from driving off!

Well, I recovered from my ring fiasco and Nadine never found out what I really was doing that day. A few weeks later, over a romantic dinner with flowers and wine, I asked her to marry me. If she only knew.

—*George Easton, San Diego, CA*

WHAT'S FOR DINNER?

$a$dam and I had been living together for some time, so I was hoping he would pop the question soon. I didn't think he could completely surprise me because I knew it was going to happen—I just didn't know when.

One night, I came home from work and asked him to go to the grocery store with me. He agreed and off we went. All we bought was frozen food, so when we got home, I put everything away in the freezer and started to walk out of the kitchen. Adam turned to me and said, "Oh no! I think we forgot to get butter." I said, "We have plenty of butter." He firmly said he didn't think so, so I went to the refrigerator to prove him wrong.

When I opened the door, I saw roses and a card inside. I was so surprised! I took the flowers out, kissed him, and prepared a vase with water for the roses. He gave me a strange look and said, "Aren't you going to open the card?" I was so excited that he had given me flowers that I had forgotten all about the card. On it he had written, "I want to spend the rest of my life with you. Will you marry me?"

I immediately turned around and there he was, kneeling on one knee on our kitchen floor, holding a beautiful ring. I couldn't have been more surprised and of course I said yes.

It turns out that the only reason he agreed to go to the grocery store was to force me to open the refrigerator when we got home! Some people have stories of limos, romantic getaways, and fancy dinners on the town, but I had a proposal I wouldn't have traded for the world.

—*Candi Gershon, Yonkers, NY*

EAT, DRINK, AND BE MARRIED

Simon and I had been together for nearly three years and were enjoying our life together. Around our third-year anniversary, I had the opportunity to travel to England. I thought it would be the perfect time for Simon to meet my relatives. Unfortunately, Simon was unable to go because he had to take a last-minute university course the exact week that I was travelling. I went to London, feeling guilty and disappointed that I had left him behind.

On my second day in England, my aunt convinced me to attend a relative's birthday party with her at the famous London pub, The Old Bull and Bush. When we arrived, nobody was there except for my cousin Ben, whom I had not seen for several years. Ben insisted on buying me a pint of Guinness, and being the beer lover I am, I couldn't turn him down.

Relatives of mine started to stream in for the party. I chatted with them as I consumed the pint of beer while sitting by the fireplace in the old pub. When I finished my beer, I noticed something shiny in my glass. At first, I thought it was a pop-can tab. However, when I held the glass up, I realized that it was a ring. I assumed the barmaid had dropped it in my drink by accident. I was about to flag her down, when Simon approached me from the bar.

I have never been so confused in my life. I tried to grasp the fact that it was really Simon. Then he got down on one knee and proposed to me. Of course, I said yes, though I had a million questions for him about why he was in London.

It turned out that he had caught a flight to London the day after me. And, while I was blissfully enjoying my Guinness during the party, he was watching the whole scene through a hole in a newspaper he pretended to read just a few feet away.

The perfect part of this proposal was that Simon and I spent the whole week in England, and he met my entire family. It was like having a honeymoon before the wedding. If you ever go to The Old Bull and Bush, look for a plaque on the wall that tells our story.

—*Susan Howarth, Ontario, Canada*

POETRY IN MOTION

*O*n Christmas Day 1997, I went to dinner at O'Hanas—a restaurant at Walt Disney World's Polynesian Resort—with my boyfriend, Jym. This restaurant holds a very special place in my heart because when I was young my family dined there. I fondly remember sitting with my father and drinking non-alcoholic tropical drinks just so I could score the little umbrellas.

This Christmas Day visit to the restaurant proved to be even more memorable. After dinner, the "Big Kahuna"—the restaurant's resident singer—serenaded me with "The Hawaiian Wedding Song." As he finished, all of the restaurant's wait-staff encircled our table. One waiter carried a huge basket of six and a half dozen roses—one rose for each month of the six and a half years Jym and I had been together. Another waiter carried a black platter with a glass slipper on it. Inside the glass slipper was a beautiful three-quarter carat diamond marquis ring.

As I turned to face Jym, he got down on one knee. He then recited this poem, which he had written:

You are my heavens, full of life and wonders. The fulfillment of every wish ever wished upon the stars you hold so gently . . .

You are my gravity, heavy and holding with your power over everything causing the tides to ebb and flow perpetually . . .

You are my moon, so beautiful and reflective, a shining inspiration in the night and a constant test of my sanity . . .

You are my sunrise, so warm and nurturing. A gentle kiss in the morning and the only one who still inspires faith in me . . .

*But of all the things that you are to me, there is still one I'd have you
be. So on this night I'll ask you please, be my wife and marry me.*

I threw my arms around Jym and euphorically said, "Yes." Everyone
in the restaurant cheered, and the manager poured us a glass of champagne. We toasted this wondrous occasion as fireworks erupted over
Cinderella's Castle. Jym really combined our love of Disney with my
Cinderella fantasy proposal—one that represents our past, present, and
future together.

—*Holly Fuhrman, Orlando, FL*

IF AT FIRST YOU DON'T SUCCEED

a few months before my eighteenth birthday, my boyfriend joined the Navy. While he was away, we talked almost daily, occasionally discussing marriage though we didn't make any definite plans. During one of these conversations, he asked my ring size. He said he wanted to get his naval graduation ring sized to my finger so I could wear it. But I was convinced that he wanted to know because he was going to buy me an engagement ring. I even went so far as to confide in my girlfriends and family.

Several months and many conversations later, he came home for his first leave. The night he returned, he had dinner at my home. After dinner, he suggested we go for a walk in the park. I agreed and winked knowingly at my family, thinking that this was it.

We walked and talked for about half an hour. Finally, we stopped and he said, "I have something for you." He handed me a black velvet ring box. I tried to act cool. I opened the box and saw . . . his graduation ring. I was very disappointed but tried to hide it. I said, "Oh, thanks" and shoved the box in my pocket.

My boyfriend offered to carry the box for me so that I wouldn't drop it. Angrily, I handed it back to him. We walked a little farther and he asked, "Did you read the inscription?" Of course, I hadn't. He suggested we stand under the streetlight so I could read it clearly. He gave the box back to me, but this time, when I opened it, it wasn't the graduation ring. It was a beautiful engagement ring.

—*Carole Holland, Jersey City, NJ*

TWICE-BAKED PROPOSAL

J was proposed to twice in my life. The first time, I doubted the sincerity of the proposal. I was working at a shoe store in Madison, Wisconsin—my summer job—when a customer became enamored with me. For about a two-week period, he would stop by every day with a friend. He never asked me out on a date, but continued his pattern of engaging me in small talk. One day, that pattern took a strange and a rather scary turn. He was talking to me, as per his M.O., when he got down on one knee and proposed to me. I was thinking that a) this man is psychotic, b) I am on candid camera, or c) this is a fraternity rite of passage. My multiple-choice quiz was never answered because after I gently turned him down I never saw him again. Come to think of it, he never bought any shoes, either.

The second time I was proposed to, I decided to accept. I had been dating my boyfriend for five years and living with him for four of those, and I must admit I wasn't really expecting a proposal of marriage. We had rather prided ourselves on having a committed, trusting relationship without the complications of marriage. Not that a wedding was out of the question—it was just not a priority.

On leap day four years ago, I returned home from working out at the local gym. My boyfriend said that he wanted to speak to me before we had dinner. There was a grave tone in his voice so I thought he was upset with me. Quite the contrary! As we sat down on the couch in our tiny New York City apartment, he looked at me and began to tell me what a wonderful person I was. I must admit that once he was through with his speech, I was pretty convinced that I was quite a catch. I still hadn't really clued in on why he was telling me all these things, until he pulled out the ring. There it was, a silver ring with an amethyst stone. Okay, now I understood. After all of those years of not really caring about proposals, weddings, and what not, I was the one caught speechless. No "yes," no witty remark, no crying, all I could manage to do was nod my head up and down.

I spent the rest of the evening listening to how he planned his proposal. First, he had picked leap day because it was in between my birthday and our anniversary. Second, he had acquired the ring in a rather unorthodox fashion. He and two single male friends went down to Greenwich Village to buy the ring. The only problem—none of them really knew what they were doing. My boyfriend had picked out a wedding band and was about to purchase it, when one of his mates said, "Hey, isn't it supposed to have a diamond or something on it?" The saleslady confirmed this assessment. When they looked at the array of diamond rings, however, they came to a second conclusion— diamond rings are really expensive. We didn't have much money, so spending a small fortune on a diamond ring was out of the question.

Tired and confused, all three of them despondently walked out of the store into the street, not knowing what to do next. It had started to rain. The same mate from before queried my boyfriend, "What's her birthstone?" Eureka! A solution had been found! In the rain, three single, tired, confused men stumbled up to a Greenwich Village street vendor and asked to see his amethyst rings. My boyfriend picked one out, and $18 later he had purchased the perfect ring. Believe it or not, this ring story brought tears to the eyes of some of our closest friends. (I guess they're easily amused.)

Even though my boyfriend was not the best prepared, I give him credit for creativity. I loved my proposal, I love my engagement ring, I love him, and I love living in wedded bliss.

—*Anonymous*

WHEN JULIE MET BRIAN

*O*ne night during my freshman year at college, I attended a fraternity party and indulged a bit too much. I was escorted back to my dorm by one of the fraternity pledges who was instructed to get me home safe and sound. This is how I met my best friend, Brian.

Over the next five years, our relationship continued to grow and flourish. We went on trips together (either with a group of friends or entirely alone), we visited each other's parents annually, befriended each other's current boyfriend or girlfriend, and remained a constant source of support and unyielding loyalty to one another. We took almost all of our classes together, played stupid competitive games, had a few spats, went to parks for long talks or walks, and generally made each other feel complete.

After college, I moved a half-hour down the coast and Brian soon followed with all his roommates. We continued our friendship, now making Tuesday nights our "date night," reserving that evening each week to catching up, gossiping, and just spending time in the other's presence.

About a year ago (nine years into our friendship), our talks became more serious. Brian began to talk about marriage, children, and what he wanted in his future wife. He even asked me if I would have his children, no matter who I married. I jokingly said I would, but soon began to think seriously about my feelings for him. A few months later on "date night," I finally asked if he could ever feel romantic about me. I asked him if we would be missing out if we didn't end up together. He said that he couldn't be with me because I was too much—too complicated and too scary for him, whatever that meant.

Four months ago, on "date night," our friendship and love for each other finally moved to another level. Brian looked up at me with clear green eyes and told me that he did not want to live a life without me—that no one he knew had a relationship like ours, a partnership filled with genuine camaraderie, love for family, passion, spirit for life, mutual respect, and admiration. He wanted us to be together forever, to not just take a chance and try, but to actually make a serious decision.

We decided to take that chance, and from that day forward everything fell beautifully into place. We took a couple of trips together right away bringing us closer together. He loved to give me momentos of these adventures. In Puerto Vallarta, he picked up a rock and gave it to me "to remember this time." In San Felipe, he gave me a seashell "to remember this day" with him.

On a trip to Boston to meet up with his family, he hired a white limousine and took me around Marblehead Neck to sightsee. When we stopped at the lighthouse, he picked up a rock. He asked what I thought of keeping it to remember the moment. I said it was "too damn big for my purse." He looked around for another rock while I took pictures.

I heard him murmur "I love you," and as I turned around, he asked me what I thought of another large rock he was holding. As I was about to comment on the girth of that one also, he dropped to one knee, turned the crystallized rock over and asked, "Will you marry me?" Inside the rock was a custom-made engagement ring sitting in a bed of cotton. It was simply the most beautiful moment of my life.

I have never seen eyes so filled with emotion and love as his were. My whole body began to shake. When he asked again, I could barely answer, thinking only, *How could I possibly be so lucky to marry the one person who, for ten years, has helped make my sun rise every morning and set every evening while just getting that much better every year?* But I managed to say yes, my heart overflowing with the love I felt.

We arrived in Boston an hour later and went to the Four Seasons Hotel, where his father had arranged for us to be given the royal treatment. It was truly an amazing day.

I'm really looking forward to our wedding day, when my best friend and I will embark on the second decade of our friendship, this time as husband and wife.

—Julie Ann Hatcher, Newport Beach, CA

SEA OF LOVE

*M*y husband and I met on a Royal Caribbean Cruise. After we'd been dating for a while, I came home one evening to a very romantic display: roses, balloons, a bottle of wine from the Royal Caribbean Cruise ship, and a detailed model of the ship, which he had built himself. At this point, I had no idea why there was such a beautiful arrangement. All I could think was "great, another thing to dust." As we looked at the ship, he showed me how the lights in the hallway gave off the same green glow as the lights on the real ship. I was really amazed at how much work he put into the model. He told me that if I opened the top of the ship, I could see all the wiring for the lights. When I opened the top, I spotted a beautiful engagement ring. I was shocked, but managed to say yes to his proposal. We were married this past May, and yes, we went on a cruise for our honeymoon.

—*Melissa King, Rumford, RI*

WEST END BOULEVARD

*O*n our first date, Steve took me for a drive down West End Boulevard in New Orleans. Suddenly, he pulled over and parked the car. He then turned to me and asked, "How about a drink, Sweetie?" Steve pulled a bottle of chilled champagne and two glasses from the back seat. We sat there in the car, parked in front of someone's house on West End Boulevard, drinking champagne and talking while the cars drove past us.

Since that date, Steve and I have been very happy together and he has never lost that romantic streak. In fact, each month he takes me out to dinner and presents me with a gift in honor of our first date. These gifts are small and always under $10.

On one such occasion, we were celebrating the anniversary of our first date by dining at my favorite restaurant. Upon leaving the restaurant, we drove down West End Boulevard to our next destination. Once again, Steve pulled over, parked the car in front of the same house, and asked, "How about a drink, Sweetie?"

While laughing and making comments about this being such a great place to have a drink, Steve reached into the back seat and presented me with a gift-wrapped box. Assuming it was my monthly anniversary gift, I unwrapped it and discovered a clear acrylic ring box containing a diamond solitaire. Expecting to receive anything else but an engagement ring, I screamed and dropped the ring box.

Steve laughed at my reaction, then reached down to retrieve the box, which he had definitely spent more than $10 on. Steve took the ring out of its box, held my hand, and asked, "Will you marry me?" After regaining my composure, I said, "Yes!" Of course, the one time that I really needed a drink, Steve did not have the champagne chilled and waiting in the back seat.

Twelve years, two children, and a dog later, Steve and I are still together. And to this day, whenever I am on West End Boulevard, I can still hear Steve clearly asking, "Will you marry me?" And I always say "Yes!" For on that night, all those years ago, Steve not only became my fiancé, but also my best friend, my confidante, my rock of stability, and much more. He is my husband, a wonderful father, and truly the love of my life.

—Denise A. Schmidt, Metairie, LA

COMING ATTRACTIONS

*M*y marriage proposal was traditional, but I received my engagement ring in a unique way. Rod, my then boyfriend, and I picked out our rings together. I was quite anxious to get my ring as quickly as possible, but Rod wanted to surprise me.

One night, while at the movies, I felt what I thought was a prize in my popcorn. I was shocked when I realized that it was actually my engagement ring. I started laughing and crying at the same time.

On August 25, 1999, Rod and I celebrated our thirty-seventh wedding anniversary. We have three daughters, one son, five granddaughters, and two grandsons. And we still enjoy a good box of popcorn every now and then.

—*Barbara Nunez, Slidell, LA*

I'LL TREASURE YOU ALWAYS

$\mathcal{M}$y girlfriend, Sherry, and I planned a romantic trip to Cozumel, Mexico, which I thought would be a perfect place to propose to her. Wanting the proposal to be unique and unforgettable, I planned an engaging scuba dive.

I arrived in Mexico three days before Sherry, along with my friend, David. We scouted underwater proposal locations and discovered a site that was thirty feet off the southwest side of the island.

After discovering the perfect spot, I began to assemble a treasure to place in an antique-looking chest. The most important items were two scrolled messages on canvas and a small round metal box containing about forty plastic pearls, a silver wedding bell for a charm bracelet, and four rings of various designs.

On Friday morning, David and I swam to some caves that were near the location where I wanted to propose. We hid the chest and piled rocks over it to obscure it from other divers. When we returned to shore, I immediately drove to the airport to meet Sherry. Wanting to do the deed before somebody happened upon the chest, I suggested to Sherry that we go for a shallow dive as soon as possible. I was worried that she might not be in a diving mood after such a long trip, but thankfully she was fine with the idea. We returned to the hotel, unpacked her bags, rounded up the scuba gear, and headed to the site.

When we began to put on our scuba diving gear, I nonchalantly signaled David (who had been keeping an eye on us from shore). Luckily, Sherry did not notice this exchange. David's mission was to swim out ahead of us, uncover the chest, and place it in a more obvious, prearranged location.

About a minute after David went in, Sherry and I submerged. In order to give David a head start, I constantly distracted Sherry while we swam by pointing out fish, coral, and an old canon from a ship wreck (basically, anything I could find). As we approached the cave's entrance, I motioned for Sherry to follow me inside. Once inside, we swam toward a shaft of light, which was the cave's exit.

As I rounded the corner to exit, I saw that David was still setting up the chest. I immediately turned Sherry around, and we swam back inside the cave. I only sidetracked Sherry momentarily, and we headed toward the exit once again. Much to my relief, David was gone.

The water was very dirty around the chest, however, because David's movements had stirred up a lot of sand. Sherry swam right past the chest. I very deliberately pointed at it. She looked at me quizzically and then swam away. I forged ahead, scooped up the chest, and swam after Sherry. I found her looking like she was searching for something or someone. I couldn't figure out what she was doing at first, but I eventually realized that she must have seen David and was desperately trying to figure out why he was there and where he went. (In actuality, David was hiding in the darkness of the cave so as not to disturb our magic moment.)

I again dramatically tried to get Sherry to focus on the chest. I fumbled with the chain. No reaction. I pried at the lock. No reaction. Finally, I opened the lid and let the some of the contents spill out. Limited reaction. I figured I was going to have to do everything for her, so I unraveled the first scroll and handed it to her. It read, "I found my treasure when I found you. Will you marry me?" No reaction. She handed it back to me and continued her search for David.

Not knowing that she hadn't actually read the first scroll, I was perplexed by her disinterest in my proposal. But I decided to plow ahead in the face of this blow and handed her the second scroll. It read, "My love for you is forever, but this ring is only temporary.

Now, you have the key to my heart." (This referred to the rings in the center of the small metal box. I didn't want to bring the real ring underwater for fear of losing it.) Finally, a real reaction.

Sherry motioned that she wanted to reread the first message, so I handed it back to her. I then reached inside the chest and took out the metal box containing the four rings. I opened the box and out poured cascading pearls, which I had placed inside the box just for this beautiful effect. I could tell that Sherry was surprised and amazed. Her eyes were moist under her goggles, and she shook her head yes, accepting my underwater proposal. I then let her pick a ring from the box, placed it on her finger, and motioned for us to surface.

When we surfaced, we exchanged a few brief words and kissed. David tentatively came out of the cave to congratulate us. We then gathered the chest and everything that had toppled out of it and swam back to shore.

—Stephen Previtera, Richmond, VA

McRING

My fiancé is a restaurant manager at McDonald's. One afternoon, he asked me to meet him there for lunch. When I arrived, he gave me a kiss and quickly took me outside to the front of the restaurant. I got the shock of my life as I looked up and saw on the big sign under the golden arches the words, "Joél, will you marry me?" As I turned to him, he pulled a French fries–shaped Limoges box from behind his back and handed it to me. I opened it and inside was a beautiful emerald cut engagement ring! I happily said yes, as he slipped the ring on my finger. We took pictures and the many people who went to McDonald's that day joined in the celebration.

—*Joél Weibelt, New Orleans, LA*

THE PERFORMANCE OF A LIFETIME

$\mathcal{B}$efore becoming engaged, Gene and I were both professional performers. Although it was an exciting life, it kept us separated much of the time. Around the time of my birthday, two years into our relationship, I was working in New York City and he was in Akron, Ohio. He happened to be working at the same theater where we had first met as the leads in *Seven Brides for Seven Brothers*.

Because my birthday happened to fall on a mutual day off, I decided to fly out to Akron to spend it with him. I booked the earliest possible flight, and took a 4:00 A.M. bus to the airport. By the time I arrived in Ohio, I was exhausted. All I wanted to do was take a nap, but Gene had other ideas. He kept talking about going on a picnic and claimed he had the perfect spot in mind. Tired as I was, I realized that for some reason this picnic was important to him. I stifled my yawns as we drove to a local park built around an old canal.

The park was really quite beautiful, and I was looking forward to spreading our blanket on the ground and eating the lovely picnic lunch he had prepared. I also planned to enjoy the warmth of the late summer sun and take an alfresco birthday nap. But again, Gene had other ideas. He insisted that the ideal spot he had found was off the beaten path, and much more private.

Now, I am not particularly fond of the outdoors. I love a garden, adore a picnic in a park, and even can handle hiking on a well-marked, well-traveled path on occasion. But that's about as far as I go. To reach Gene's perfect spot, we fought through some undergrowth, traversed a stream without the aid of a bridge, and trudged through the woods. Through all this, Gene carried his guitar. About halfway through this adventure, I was thinking to myself, *Why are we doing this? It's my birthday, and I hate this stuff!* Still, it seemed very important to Gene that we continue on this journey.

We finally emerged onto a secluded embankment overlooking a branch of the river. At once, I understood why Gene wanted me to see this part of the park. We were surrounded by nature's beauty and were completely alone. The details of the meal are lost to me, but I remember that it all tasted wonderful. When we finished eating, Gene pulled out his guitar.

Music has always been an important part of our relationship, so part of my birthday lunch was a concert of all the songs that were special to us. I laid back on the blanket and listened to this man who I loved so much serenade me with songs full of powerful emotions. The impromptu concert and intimate setting combined to make my birthday a day to remember forever.

At one point, Gene said, "I have a new song to play for you. I learned it just for today." He began to play, but for some reason he faltered and had to stop. I asked, "Sweetheart, why are you so nervous? It's just me." He then started to play again. It was the most beautiful rendition of Richard Marx's "Now and Forever."

When he finished playing, I leaned over and kissed him. He then slipped a ring box between us. I opened it and saw the beautiful ring he had designed. He asked me to marry him. As soon as I said yes, we both started crying.

At that moment, two cranes—birds that mate for life and are used to symbolize fidelity in Asian art and literature—lifted off from the river below us. Overhead they squawked once, as if to wish us happiness in our new life. It was a special and prophetic moment for both of us.

Later that night, at an elegant romantic dinner, Gene told me he had written to my parents to ask for their blessing and had the ring designed to match a beautiful white gold antique wedding band he'd bought earlier.

Our beautiful wedding took place in a park in my hometown. It was on the shores of the lake where I used to ice skate as a child. We paid for it and our incredible three-week honeymoon in Ireland with some of the money I had won as a contestant on *Wheel of Fortune*. (No, he didn't marry me for the money—or so he says.)

—*Amy Connor, New York, NY*

A HOLE IN ONE

$\mathcal{I}$t was New Year's Day and I was at the Rose Bowl with a few of my friends. Kickoff was still two hours away, so while tailgating by our car in the parking lot (which was actually a golf course covered with parked cars), they took a golf club out from the trunk and began to putt balls into a plastic cup thirty feet away.

While waiting my turn, I struck up a conversation with three guys sitting on the grass next to a nearby car. Being a huge sports fan, I was having a great time talking about college football and basketball. One guy in the group, Eric, couldn't believe that a female actually knew something about sports. He focused all his attention on me. I wasn't dating anyone at the time, so I looked at the situation as a great way to meet a new man. Eric's sweet personality and great sense of humor were the perfect antidote to my holiday doldrums.

He glanced over at my friends who were still putting away and asked me, "Are you going to take a putt?" I said that I was thinking about it, and he said, "I'll tell you what. If you sink that putt, I'll get down on my knee right here and propose to you. I've never met a woman who can talk sports like you." I thought this was an interesting compliment with a lot of potential, but I didn't know if he was serious or not. I took my chances.

My turn came and so began my attempt at getting engaged. Okay, so I had known the guy for only ten minutes, but it was the best offer I had received in a long time. I stood on the "putting green" with six balls to work with. Eric was telling everyone how much he wanted me to make it, so all of the people around our car began to cheer me on. Unfortunately, the first three putts went to the right of the cup and the next three went to the left. My friend decided to toss me one more ball to make it a lucky seventh shot. I carefully lined up the ball, took a swing, and laughed as the ball rolled right into the cup— a solid hole in one. Everyone applauded as Eric strolled over to me. He got down on one knee, took my hand, kissed it, and said, "Be my wife?" I chuckled and replied, "Only if you tell me your last name first!"

—*Anonymous*

DÉJÀ VU

$\mathcal{I}$t was September 22, but I hadn't planned on asking my girlfriend, Christie, to marry me until mid-October. However, when the ring I had ordered came in that day, I took off from work a little early to pick it up. When I finally saw the diamond, something clicked inside me. The ring was beautiful and I decided I was going to give it to her that night.

It was about 4:45 P.M. when I left the jewelry store. Christie was going to be at my place in about two hours, so I had to think fast. Originally, I made reservations at a romantic Italian restaurant in Fort Worth. I called them back two minutes later to change the time, and two minutes later to cancel—inspiration had struck! We would re-create our first date.

I couldn't remember the name of the place we went on our first date, so I couldn't call for reservations. I did, however, remember where it was, so I drove there at breakneck speed, ran in, and made a walk-in reservation. It was called the City Park Café. They looked at me a bit oddly, but wrote down my reservation anyway. Next, I called the Tandy Center Ice Skating Rink, another place we went on our first date. They were closed for a special competition, so my plans were foiled. Time was running out and I still didn't have a proposal strategy!

It was now 6:00 P.M., and Christie was supposed to be arriving in about an hour. I had given the proposal a lot of thought prior to that afternoon, but all of my plans had fallen through. Finally, inspiration hit again at 6:45. I gathered up the necessary items and put them in the car. I ran back to get the ring and put it in my pocket. As I was getting into the car to get her some roses, Christie drove up.

She asked where I was going and I told her I had to get something at the store. Fortunately, she was still in her work clothes and wanted to change. She said she would just stay at my place. I went to the store and picked up the roses, but then realized I should find another item because she would probably ask why I went to the store. So I got some contact lens solution.

The first thing she asked when I walked in was not, "What did you get at the store?" but rather, "Who are the roses for?" I told her they were for her, and she asked why. I said that we were going to be celebrating her birthday again. Her birthday was the month before at a period of time when I was particularly broke. I had gotten her a couple of things, but promised I would get her something better in September.

I explained we were going to go somewhere fun for dinner and that I had a little gift for her. I warned her that she shouldn't get too excited because it wasn't that big of a deal. This seemed to satisfy her and got me off the hook for the rest of the evening.

We then took off to City Park Café. When we arrived, the owner recognized me and said "For you, we have the best seat in the house." Not a bad touch, but I suppose it had to do with the fact that he didn't get very many walk-in reservations.

After a great dinner, we moved on to "Operation Forever." Part of my birthday present to Christie, I explained, was to walk down memory lane. I began to reminisce about our first date and about our adventures since then—very romantic stuff.

We then drove to the campus of Texas Christian University (of which we are both alumni) and parked in front of Frog Fountain (a famous TCU landmark). We got out of the car and I grabbed a bag in which there was a book about the history of TCU. Inside the book I had placed a purple ribbon that was tied to a little bag.

We walked over to Frog Fountain and I nervously handed Christie the book and said, "Would you like to make a little more TCU history with me?" She gave me this very puzzled look until she noticed the bag attached to the ribbon. She opened the bag and then she started shaking and breathing strangely.

Christie managed to get the box out of the bag, but couldn't seem to open it. She tried opening every side but the correct one. When she finally opened the box and saw the ring, I asked simply, "So, will you marry me?" She says she said "Yes," but I just remember her putting on the ring and hugging me.

—Joshua Harmon, Fort Worth, TX

LONDON CALLING

*M*y boyfriend and I were on vacation in London last August. Near the end of our trip, he begged me to go for one last walk in Hyde Park. I was feeling a bit homesick and just wanted to stay at the hotel, but his eagerness convinced me that I should go. When we arrived at the park, we walked to Kensington Palace and around a nearby pond. He pointed at the full moon and the swans that were swimming in the pond. It was a beautiful sight. As we stood in that perfect place at this perfect time, he slipped the ring onto my finger and proposed. Of course, I said yes—and my homesickness melted away.

—*Jody Nelson, Bridgeport, WA*

CANDID CAMERA

$\mathcal{M}$y boyfriend, Wayne, and I met while taking a comedy writing class at the Acme comedy theater. We knew right away that we would get married eventually and talked about it often. Once in awhile, I would ask how long he wanted to wait before getting married. He would only answer, "Don't worry, it'll be soon."

He was spending a lot of time in Orange County playing basketball and hanging out with his friends. It made for some lonely days, but it was also usually on days when I was working as a tour guide at Universal Studios. I wasn't angry, but I did miss seeing him.

On the anniversary of our first date, we had made plans to go out. I told him I couldn't afford to get him a gift, so we decided not to exchange gifts—he would just plan a romantic dinner for two.

On the day of our big date, we drove to Orange County. Wayne was unusually quiet, and at one point he kind of shivered. I asked him if he was okay and he said he was just remembering the taste of this awful three-bean salad he had eaten (boy, was I oblivious). I kept asking him where we were going, but he kept it a secret. We finally pulled into his best friend Pat's driveway. We walked right up to the front door and he opened it without knocking. I said, "Wayne, we can't just go in. . . . What are you doing?" He just laughed.

No one was in the house, but a big movie screen and video projector were set up in the living room. I was confused by the setup. Then Wayne turned on the projector and asked me to sit down. He had compiled a video of himself, reminiscing to me about the past year. It began as "Video Wayne" asked "Real-life Wayne" to take a piece of paper out of his pocket and read it to me. He was shaky as he read the words, "Genevieve, I love you." My stomach was in knots and I was crying.

"Video Wayne" said, "What a great year this has been! Here's another look at it with pictures and music, so just sit back and enjoy." The rest of the video consisted of photographs of the two of us, and of Wayne driving around to our favorite places set to music. When it was done, "Video Wayne" told "Real-life Wayne" to give me a kiss and take me outside. Pat and two other friends, Warren and Tim, were in the backyard. They had set up a drum set, guitar, keyboards, and a microphone for Wayne to sing. A chair had been set up for me to sit and watch.

He sang two songs for me—"Jenny (867-5309)," which is my nickname and the first message he ever left for me on my answering machine, and "Can't Take My Eyes Off of You," which became "our song" on our first date when we sang it at the top of our lungs on the way home from dinner.

I was bawling. He took my hand and got down on one knee. "Genevieve," he said. I shouted, "I love you!" He stepped back and said, "Genevieve, will you marry me?" In a millisecond, I replied yes, as I hugged and kissed him over and over (he taped the whole thing and later put it on a tape with our wedding).

We went out for dinner afterward and I was so excited I couldn't eat. On the way home, I had to ask him to pull over, because I leaned out of the car and threw up—twice. Boy meets girl, boy proposes to girl, girl pukes!

It turns out that all the time Wayne was supposedly playing basketball, he was really filming the video. He still sings to me every now and then, and no, I didn't throw up on our wedding day!

—*Genevieve (Terich) Miller, Pasadena, CA*

I JUST WANT TO BE YOUR TEDDY BEAR

J had known Neil for just five short months. We had a long-distance relationship, which had managed to survive and thrive on phone calls and two short visits totaling ten days.

Near the end of Neil's second visit, we traveled to Sydney, Australia, to take in a show and enjoy the sights and sounds of the big city. After the show, we walked on the waterfront of Sydney's beautiful harbor. As we walked, I noticed that Neil was holding a large plastic bag under his arm. When I asked him what it was, Neil simply said that it was a present for me.

We approached a park bench and sat down. By now, my curiosity was piqued. Neil handed me the bag and, as I opened it, he got down on one knee. I lifted the present out of the bag—a cute, fluffy teddy bear. As I looked at the bear, I noticed a gold necklace around its neck. Hanging from the chain was a tiny toy ring. Then, on perfect cue, Neil asked me to be his wife.

I was stunned because we had been together for only a short while, but in my heart I knew that I had found my God-given partner. With a smile and nervous giggle, I answered, "Yes." Neil then slipped the little ring onto my finger.

I am proud to say that I continued to wear that $3.50 ring until I received the "real" one a month later. We are now happily married. And at the head of our bed sits the teddy bear with that small tarnished ring hanging from its neck. It serves as a reminder of that unique night when our love turned into a lifelong commitment.

—*Fiona Foyster, Queanbeyan, Australia*

IT MUST HAVE BEEN SOMETHING I SAID

J had just about given up on dating when I met Joe. We met through an online dating service and fell in love almost immediately. We both knew exactly what we were looking for in a mate. As we got to know each other we discovered that we had the same values, morals, and tastes.

I am a single mother of an eleven-year-old and was working full-time, going to school full-time, and being a mother full-time. I did my best to work around my daughter's schedule so that I could enjoy every free minute I had with her. Joe was completely understanding of this and so much more. If I couldn't see him all week, he would very patiently wait until I had some free time, completely taking all of the pressure off of me.

Now, Joe had made up this little ditty about me and had been singing it to me almost since the day we met. It went like this, "Susan Jayne . . . love of my life . . . soon to be my wife." But he never officially asked me to marry him.

When I was close to graduating with my bachelor's degree, I was busier than ever. I had several papers due and exams every week, so I spent most of my free time at the library studying. As a result, Joe and I did not get to spend much time together. But Joe was right there with my daughter, both of them offering me their full support.

Soon after graduation in May, he took me away to a really nice hotel for the night. We had talked about getting away for a night together for quite some time so I had no idea that he had something extra special planned.

While I was in the shower, Joe lit up the entire hotel room with candles. When I sat down on the couch, he got down on one knee next to me, and shaking like a leaf, sang, "Susan Jayne . . . love of my life . . . will you be my wife?"

Of course, I said yes. I have never once doubted our relationship and knew right from the start that Joe was my soulmate for life. I love him more than life itself and have never been happier!

—*Sue Doucette, Tewksbury, MA*

A KAYAK BUILT FOR TWO

$\mathcal{M}$att and I had been together for about a year and a half. We didn't spend much time alone together, because I have a two-year-old daughter from a previous marriage. So when Matt suggested a kayak trip for the two of us, I jumped at the opportunity.

We live in Bayfield, Wisconsin—way up on the south shore of Lake Superior. There are twenty-two Apostle Islands, but the only one I had ever been to was Madeline, and only because I work there. I have always wanted to see some of the other islands. Matt, on the other hand, has worked as a kayak guide for six years, taking trips out to the various islands, so he was very familiar with most of them.

I let Matt make all of the plans for our trip. He went around for days muttering about which side of which island would have the best sunset versus sunrise, where you could get the best view of the other islands, and if I wanted to see sea caves or shipwrecks or both. He finally got it all figured out, but wouldn't tell me anything about where we were going.

Matt had everything packed and ready to go. (I let him do it all because he was the pro.) It was a beautiful day, and the lake was fairly calm. I was in the front of the kayak, so when the waves swelled four- to five-feet high, I got drenched. Lake Superior is very cold in September. We made it to camp just in time to watch the sun set.

The next morning, Matt was up with the sun. He had made a fire and was boiling water for coffee. I am pretty grumpy in the morning until I have my coffee, so he was trying to cheer me up. He was singing and dancing around the tent trying to make me laugh and get up. It was still pretty early, and all I wanted to do was sleep.

Once the coffee was ready, he persuaded me to get up. I was sitting by the fire, trying to get warm when Matt stood up and started walking toward the beach. After about five minutes, he called me to him. When I got there, he put his arms around me and we stood watching the sunrise. The lake was so calm it looked like glass, and the reflection of the sunrise on the water was beautiful.

Suddenly, Matt said, "Put down your coffee." I looked at him like he was crazy and replied, "I am not putting my coffee down." Rather than argue with me, he simply got down on one knee. I kind of gulped and said, "I'm putting my coffee down now." He then said that he loved me more than anything in the whole world and asked if I would do him the honor of becoming his wife. I got all choked up but managed to say, "Yes." We hugged and kissed for a while and then started to plan our future together.

—*Jennifer Honl, Bayfield, WI*

YOU'VE GOT MAIL

$\mathcal{M}$y boyfriend decided to leave his computer at my place, but asked that my son not use it without him being there to supervise him. The next Sunday, I went home from church and he asked me what happened to his computer. I started to panic because I had let my son use it unsupervised the night before and I thought I had been caught. Innocently, I asked my boyfriend what he meant and he requested I come and look at the computer myself. When I looked at the monitor, I saw his new screensaver, which had the words "Will you marry me?" typed in bold rainbow colors. I was delighted (and relieved), so of course I said yes.

—*La' Tanya Mathews-Law, Steger, IL*

LOVE AND WAR

*I*n early 1966, my boyfriend left for a six-month tour of duty in Vietnam. Before he left, he asked me to go steady. We exchanged high school rings—he wore mine on his pinkie because it did not fit on his ring finger.

In July 1966, I received a money order in the mail with no explanation. A few days later, a letter arrived from the army. It said that during a raid on the base where my boyfriend was stationed, my ring had slipped off his finger. It was forever lost and the money order was for me to buy a replacement.

My boyfriend came home in early December. On Saturday, December 10, 1966, he picked me up for a date. As we drove, he said that he had to stop by his parents' home for a minute. He rushed in and out so quickly that I didn't even have time to get out of the car. He jumped back in the car and we headed toward the highway. When we reached the stop sign, he pulled over and gave me a little box. I opened the box and could barely believe my eyes—he had replaced my lost ring with a diamond engagement ring that he had brought back from Vietnam. I was so stunned that it was hard for me to find the words to accept his proposal. But I did.

Because he had another tour of duty in Southeast Asia, we did not get married until May 1968. We recently celebrated our thirty-first anniversary.

—Brenda Portinari, Jefferson, LA

CHANGE OF PLANS

$\mathcal{I}$ met my husband, Brent, in a history class during my senior year of college. We quickly became friends, and eventually that friendship grew into something more and we began dating.

After graduation, I went to work for a CPA firm and Brent started working part time for Prudential Health. One February, Brent told me that he wanted me to go with him to a company convention in Arizona in June. I got the vacation time, and throughout the hectic tax season all I could think about was how nice this getaway in Arizona was going to be.

June arrived and I was all set. Never having been to Arizona, I researched all the places to see, restaurants to eat at, baseball games to watch, and natural monuments to visit. In other words, I had planned a truly "touristy" visit and had told all of my friends and family how excited I was to get away with Brent.

We arrived at the airport for our 9:00 A.M. flight in plenty of time. As we waited in line to check in, we talked about the plans I had made. Right before we reached the counter, Brent asked me to go to the restroom to get him some tissues because his nose was running. After much persuasion, I reluctantly headed for the restrooms, which were up one floor. By the time I returned, all I had to do was show my ID and our check-in was complete.

We then decided to have breakfast. While sitting at the table, I became anxious after noticing that none of the surrounding gates listed Arizona as their flight destination—they all said Hawaii. I asked Brent which gate we were supposed to go to and he said nineteen. There was no Gate 19 anywhere near us and I got really worried, thinking we might be in the wrong terminal or that we missed the flight completely. At this point, Brent calmed me down and told me that we weren't really going to Arizona and that there was no company convention. He pulled out tons of brochures and travel books with HAWAII in big letters written on them. I was truly shocked.

We boarded our flight to Oahu and Brent said that this trip was a reward for our recent successes—his new job at Anderson Consulting and my acceptance into law school. He wanted us to really enjoy the trip and have fun. I was blown away.

Brent had arranged for us to stay at a bed and breakfast on the water for the first three days and at a condo for the last two. We spent those first few days playing in the surf, learning to snorkel, and lying in the sun without a care in the world. On Friday night, Brent had made reservations for us to have a nice dinner at a place called The Swan Court. While I was getting ready, Brent disappeared and was nowhere to be found moments before our reservation time. He finally returned with a beautiful bouquet of flowers and a wonderfully scented lei. We rushed to the restaurant and were seated on the most beautiful point overlooking waterfalls, with swans swimming in the ponds, accented by the colors of the sunset reflecting on the rocks. I was in heaven. We ordered a bottle of wine and talked while it chilled.

We discussed the events of the day and how it was so odd that we had been mistaken for a newlywed couple everywhere we had gone. I was even mistakenly called "Mrs. Hayward" by at least ten people.

About five minutes after we ordered, he excused himself to use the restroom. After ten minutes, he still hadn't returned. I started to get a little worried, but he soon appeared bearing a single red rose and a card. Immediately, I thought of our "dating" anniversary and was touched that he remembered. He told me that I couldn't open the card until after dinner.

Dinner came and went and I finally asked if I could open the card. He said okay. I opened it and it was beautifully romantic, describing his feelings for me and how he wanted to spend the rest of his life with me. I didn't think too much of it because we had already shared these feelings with each other. I was touched by the card and thanked him. Noticing the quick manner in which I read the card, put it away, and thanked him with kisses, he asked if I had read it. I said that I had. He looked at me with a funny blank stare and told me I should read it again. Befuddled, I did. Again, I thanked him for the card and for his thoughtfulness. He was truly puzzled at this point and asked me to really read it *again*. Not understanding, I read it again, and as I did he got down on one knee, took out a black box, and opened it in front of me, revealing the most brilliant diamond ring.

Now I don't remember exactly what he told me before he asked me to marry him, partly because I was in shock and partly because I was asking him a million questions. He asked me again to marry him, and again I was too shocked and confused to answer. By this time, the entire restaurant was watching, eagerly awaiting my response. Brent asked, partly out of humor and partly out of fear, "Are you going to make me ask you three times? Will you marry me?" I nodded furiously. Brent said, "Don't nod. You need to say something," to which I replied, "Yes." This response was applauded and Brent stood up with a smile. I was at a loss for words when he said, "Well, don't you want to hug me or something?" I leapt up and gave him the biggest hug ever as he put the ring on my finger.

Then I listened, between bouts of hysterical crying, as Brent explained his plan, how my parents and his parents already knew, how most of our friends already knew, and how he had this planned since February. And to think, I thought I was going to Arizona!

—*Kelli Daye Hayward, Redondo Beach, CA*

A SCARY PROPOSAL

*M*y boyfriend and I had just returned from seeing an incredibly scary horror movie, in which a man kills the woman he loves. I'm not a big fan of horror films so I was spooked for the rest of the night. I was having a difficult time falling asleep, but finally managed to drift off. Suddenly, I awoke in a panic because I felt the presence of someone hovering over me. The room was pitch black, but there was definitely a man standing over me and he was holding something. Terrified, I screamed with all my might. Then the man turned on the light. It was my boyfriend, and he was holding an engagement ring.

—Olivia James, Dayton, NJ

TAKING THE PLUNGE

$\mathcal{T}$o celebrate my birthday, I made arrangements with a group of close friends, including my boyfriend Paul, to go to Chessington World of Adventures. It is a zoo and amusement park, like Disney World on a smaller scale.

As we entered Chessington World of Adventures, a woman introduced herself to us as coordinator of the amusement park. She said that she had been contacted by Paul, who had told her that it was my birthday. Because it was my special day, she arranged for us to ride the park's new ride, the Rattlesnake, without having to wait in line. Because there is normally more than an hour wait for this ride, I thought it was a wonderful surprise.

We all walked over to the Rattlesnake and were seated immediately. The roller coaster moved only about ten feet before stopping dead. It was a very nerve-racking experience, as I thought something had broken down. Then an announcement came over the public address system: "We have a special guest here today by the name of Jane Thomas who is celebrating her birthday. So, Happy Birthday Jane." There was a pause and the announcement continued: "We also have another special guest here by the name of Paul Harle, and Jane we have a question for you: Will you marry Paul?"

I was struck speechless as the roller coaster continued its uphill climb and dropped over the other side. At that point, I saw an enormous banner across the first car of the roller coaster that read: "Jane Thomas, will you marry me? Love, Paul Harle." Paul nudged me in the ribs and said, "Well?" I was still unable to give him an answer because I was so stunned.

When the ride ended, we disembarked to a round of applause from everyone who was in line for the roller coaster. Somebody asked me what my answer had been, and I screamed "Yes!"

The amusement park also arranged for us to have a photo shoot at the Rattlesnake and gave us the pictures as a memento. Although Paul says he's not romantic, I think this proposal proves otherwise.

—*Jane Thomas, London, England*

KEEP THE HOME FIRES BURNING

*I*n 1950, I was living in an apartment that had one fireplace to keep two rooms warm. My boyfriend lived in a similar apartment. One evening, he came by to take me out. He stood by my fireplace and shyly moved the wood and coals around with the poker. As I walked by him, he took me in his arms and asked, "Don't you think one coal pile would be cheaper than two?" We married two months later.

—*Mrs. James W. Cron, Portland, TN*

SAME TIME, NEXT YEAR

*J*ennifer and I both worked at the UCLA Student Store. She was a supervisor, and I was one of her peons. One day, we happened to get off work at the same time and walked back toward the dorms together. This was the first time we had talked, and as we were about to part ways she asked if I wanted to catch a movie that night. I said yes, and we were off. This fateful day happened to be the Thursday of the first week of the winter quarter at UCLA.

Getting to know her was great, until I found out she had a boyfriend. But it was too late, I had already fallen head over heels in love with her. One afternoon at work, Jennifer asked me if I had heard. "Heard what?" I asked. She showed me her ring and told me that she had gotten engaged. I calmly said, "Congrats," turned around, clocked out, and never went in to work again.

After a few months of agonizingly trying to win over an engaged woman, I finally gave up. One afternoon, I went by the student store and asked her to go to lunch. We went to Taco Bell, our usual hangout. I eventually got up the courage to tell her that I was in love with her, but I never wanted to see her again. I didn't realize it at the time, but that day happened to be the Thursday of the first week of the winter quarter. It was exactly one year after I met her that I told her to stay out of my life.

Several months later, I was at Student Health Services waiting to be seen for a broken wrist, and in walked Jennifer. Our eyes met and we sat and talked for hours like we hadn't missed a day. After that, we became close again, but this time I told her I was content to be just a friend (okay, it was a total lie). I told her that I accepted the fact that she would marry this other guy, but asked her one favor. On the Thursday of the first week of the winter quarter—our day— I wanted to meet her at the Bruin Bear statue at noon and take her to lunch at Taco Bell. She didn't answer.

Months went by and I guess the friendship approach actually worked. She broke off her engagement and gave me a chance. It was great to finally be in her life without any distractions.

The Thursday of the first week of the winter quarter came around again and I thought that because she never really gave me an answer on our little agreement, and because she was my girlfriend now, I didn't need to meet her at the Bear for lunch. I was wrong. She was there waiting for me and later gave me hell for not showing up. I vowed not to miss it again.

A year later, that special day came again. I had graduated and was working in the South Bay and she was in school getting her teaching credential. Without having spoken a word of the reunion at the Bear since last year, I took a long lunch to see if she would be waiting—she was. As I walked toward her, I thought to myself that if she was there next year at this time, I'd arrive with a surprise.

I now knew what I had to do before the next Bear meeting came up. I searched jewelry stores across Los Angeles for just the right ring. It was really nerve-racking! After months of looking, I finally found the perfect one. It was out of my price range, but it didn't matter because she deserved the best.

This year on "our" Thursday, I left work at 11:00 A.M. to take a long lunch and possibly get engaged to the girl of my dreams. I was really worried about her making it this year because she had just started a new teaching job and hadn't earned any days off. I arrived in the UCLA parking lot and began my walk to the Bear. As I turned the corner at 12:10 P.M., I saw Jennifer waiting for me. We hadn't spoken of this day for a year and we both remembered.

I gave her a hug and told her I was glad she could make it. She confessed that she had told the school during her interview process that she needed this day off. After we talked for a few minutes, I finally mustered up some courage and dropped to my knee. Right there at the Bruin Bear, at 12:20 P.M. on the Thursday of the first week of the winter quarter in a slight drizzle, I asked her to marry me. She was speechless. Then I pulled the ring out of my sock (I put it there because she would've noticed the ring box in my pants pocket). My hands were shaking so much that the ring fell out of the box onto the Bruin Walk. I picked up the ring, put it back in the box, and asked her again. She answered with, "Are you serious? Is this a joke?" Eventually, after I convinced her that I was terribly serious, she said yes.

I got up from my knee and helped her put on the ring. We hugged and talked for a while, and then followed tradition by heading to Taco Bell to eat. We bought lunch, but then sat down and stared at each other. She started to cry and I just sat there relieved that the pressure was over. It was an amazing feeling.

—*Jason Moreno, Los Angeles, CA*

X MARKS THE SPOT

*O*ne afternoon, my boyfriend, Scott, asked me to watch his brother's kids while he and his brother worked. After about three hours, Scott came back and gave me a dozen long-stemmed roses. I thought he was just being romantic until he handed me a golf ball that had "Paul's Par Three" (a local golf course) written on it. He then took me there to play nine holes of golf—another cool surprise. When we got to the last hole, I found a note and a string with a little key on the end of it. I opened the piece of paper. The note was actually a treasure map Scott had drawn, and at the bottom it said, "Now that you have the key, unlock the door to our future." My heart started to pound.

We walked back to Scott's car and he blindfolded me. I was a bit nervous, but I trusted him completely. Once we got to our destination, he made me keep the blindfold on while he carefully led me to a place several yards away. When he took off the blindfold, the first thing I saw was fire. We were standing on the beach of the Great Salt Lake in the middle of a huge heart Scott had made out of a long rope that was lit on fire. I looked down and saw a clump of dirt with two roses crossed on top to form an X. On each side, there was a hanging glass candle holder with a lit candle inside. I couldn't believe Scott had gone to so much trouble just for me. As an added bonus, I noticed some of our friends and relatives standing nearby watching and capturing the moment on video.

Scott handed me a shovel to dig up my treasure. It didn't take very long for me to unearth a huge treasure chest, which had a lock on it that I opened with my key. Inside the chest were dozens of rose petals and a poem Scott wrote. I was feeling completely over-whelmed. As I sat in the sand, he took the poem out and read it to me.

To Cassi:
Who would've thought we'd end up together?
All I know now is I want to be with you forever.
From the first time I held your hand
I knew I couldn't stand being without you.
I never want to miss another kiss
Coming from your lips.
I think of you in the utmost respect
And I promise to always protect you.
When I look into your eyes
It makes me want to cry because I'm so lucky.
You make me truly happy
And I promise to never treat you crappy.
You are so perfect and I wouldn't change a thing,
That is why I have chosen to buy you this ring.
You make me want to take this relationship higher
Because of the way you light my heart on fire.
Love, Scott

After reading the poem, Scott asked me to stand up and he got down on one knee. My heart raced as I watched him take a rose-shaped box out of the treasure chest. He opened it to reveal a beautiful dia-mond ring, and then asked me to marry him. Of course I said yes! His proposal confirmed how lucky I am to have Scott in my life.

—*Cassi Draper, Magna, UT*

LET'S MAKE A DEAL

*F*or our annual group vacation, our friends planned a cruise to Mexico. Unfortunately, one month prior to our sailing, we saw on CNN News that the ship we were to sail on had caught on fire off the coast of Miami! Scrambling to plan an alternative excursion, my boyfriend, Ralph, booked a similar cruise for the gang on another ship. On the second night of our trip, we all attended the Captain's Cocktail Party. We were dressed in formal wear and were having a really great time. The cruise director announced a raffle just as Ralph slipped away to the restroom. I was hoping to win something, but in all the raffles I had ever entered, I'd never won. The cruise director said that there was only going to be one prize and then drew a name. It was mine! I was very excited, but a bit sad that Ralph wasn't there to share the moment with me.

My friends congratulated me and I ran onstage to collect my prize—a dozen roses and a bottle of champagne. I was then given a choice to trade them for the prize behind door #1. My friends shouted for me to pick the mystery prize, so I decided to go for it. Suddenly, the lights dimmed and out came Ralph under the spotlight. He got down on one knee and proposed to me in front of all of my dearest friends and one thousand people on board! I couldn't wait to say yes! It truly couldn't have been more perfect, and I'll treasure that moment for the rest of my life.

—*Louise Bianchi, Tampa, FL*

TAKE ME OUT TO THE BALL GAME

Sherry and I first met on a blind date. It was love at first sight. After dating for about nine months, we both agreed that we wanted to spend the rest of our lives together. We even went shopping for rings so I would know what style she liked. I bought the ring, but still had to decide how to pop the question.

I am the manager of an insurance company and an avid sports fan—especially baseball. It just so happened that my office was planning an outing to the Cubs vs. Phillies game that Saturday. I arranged for both sets of parents, mine and hers, to go to the game but to sit in a different section of the stadium. Sherry and I sat with the gang from my office.

Around the seventh inning, it was time to put my plan in motion. I had talked with the stadium management and secured their permission to use the scoreboard. At the appointed time, the screen read: "Sherry Sidwell, will you marry me? Halvo."

When Sherry saw the screen, she couldn't believe what she was reading. She started crying. Once she had caught her breath, she said yes and threw her arms around me. Our parents rushed to our side to congratulate us. My friends from the office then hung a homemade banner over the railing that said, "Jon, Sherry says yes!"

—*Jon Halvorsen, Mt. Prospect, IL*

LUCK OF THE IRISH

*I*t was New Year's Eve and we were in Northern Ireland visiting my boyfriend's parents. In the afternoon, we drove to a neighboring town to visit my grandfather. My boyfriend, Michael, suggested that on the way back we stop at a local tourist spot, one of Ireland's beautiful beaches.

Unfortunately, this was Michael's first time driving to my grandfather's house. He did not know that the gatepost at the beginning of the driveway has a formidable reputation in our family. Michael was driving his father's new car. As he started to turn into the driveway, we heard the horrible sound of grinding metal. I looked out the window just as the wing mirror was forcibly detached from the body of the car.

In December in Ireland, daylight fades rapidly in the afternoon. So, after a very short visit with my grandfather, we had to return to Michael's parents' house so that his father could assess the damage to the car in full daylight. Unfortunately, this meant that our planned side trip to the beach was canceled.

That evening, we ate a big dinner with Michael's family. Afterward, we all sat around waiting for Big Ben to chime in the New Year. At two minutes till midnight, Michael asked me to join him in the kitchen. As soon as we were alone, he went down on one knee and asked me to marry him. What else could I say but yes?

We rejoined the family in the living room, and as Big Ben chimed midnight, Michael proposed a toast to his family on behalf of himself and me—his fiancée. There was a stunned silence before the champagne corks popped.

Later that night, Michael revealed to me that his original plan had been to propose on the beach we were to visit that afternoon. After the fiasco with the car, he thought the plan had been ruined. But thankfully he made the best of it. Whatever bumps we may encounter on the road ahead, I'll always feel lucky to have found Michael.

—*Rhona Gibson, Old Aberdeen, Scotland*

PLANTING THE SEED

$\mathcal{F}$or months, my boyfriend and I had planned to have a pumpkin-carving contest between the two of us on the night before Halloween. In mid-October, we bought our pumpkins, sat them on my kitchen counter, and began the countdown to the contest. After two weeks of anticipation, October 30 finally arrived. We came home from dinner and, with much excitement, set our pumpkins on my kitchen table, ready to carve away.

Knowing I had a great chance of winning the contest, I carefully began to prepare my pumpkin. I cut the top open and began to clean out the seeds from the inside. As I was doing this, I found a little plastic container—the kind you get from a bubble gum machine with a prize inside. Confused, I opened it up and found a beautiful diamond ring! Completely baffled, I kept saying, "Oh my God—it's a ring! How did you get it in there?" Then my boyfriend got down on one knee, took my hand, and asked me to marry him. I almost cried as I said yes.

After searching the pumpkin later, I discovered that he had cut out the bottom stem, slipped the container inside, and glued the stem back on. What a creative guy!

—*Lauren Reisner, Hoboken, NJ*

IN THE NICK OF TIME

*N*ick and I dated for ten years, and I often joked that when he finally decided to propose to me, it had better be a doozie.

One rainy evening, Nick left our apartment to attend a hockey game with his friends. Shortly thereafter, I waited in our apartment building's lobby for my sister, Susan, to pick me up so that we could attend a Hollywood movie premiere. She pulled up to the curb, got out of the car as I got in, told me that she had to go to the bathroom, and quickly entered our apartment building. She was gone for quite a while, but I waited patiently in the car. When she returned, she told me that she had gone upstairs to use the bathroom in our apartment, but because no one was there, she had to use the one in the lobby. This explained why she had been gone for so long.

Finally, we were off to the screening. We arrived and were walking to the theater when Susan stopped dead in her tracks. She had forgotten the tickets. We returned to the car and Susan called her friend who had given us the tickets. Her friend said that we had to have the actual tickets in order to attend the event.

We went back to my building to search for them. Susan said she would look in the lobby restroom and suggested that I go upstairs to check the hallway outside of my apartment. As I approached my apartment door, I heard music. I knew that I had not left the stereo on, but I could not enter the apartment because I had left my keys in Susan's car. I tentatively knocked on the door.

The door opened slowly to reveal Nick, handsomely dressed in a suit. He took my hand, led me into our candlelit apartment, and guided me through ten romantic stations set up around our living and dining rooms. Each station represented one of the years we had been together and consisted of a burning candle, a framed picture of us from that year, and a mounted poem eloquently summarizing a significant event in our relationship from that year. As we proceeded from station to station, a snippet of "our song" from each year played from a cassette on the stereo.

Next, we walked outside onto our seventeenth-floor balcony. Nick handed me a poem he wrote entitled "Hand in Hand." After I read it, he turned me around to face the opposite direction. Across the street in the pouring rain stood his two best friends holding a thirty-foot banner that read "Will you marry me?"

We went back inside the apartment, and Nick got down on his knees to officially propose to me with a gold and emerald bracelet— he knew that I didn't want a separate engagement ring and wedding band. Shocked and amazed that he would go to this much trouble, I ecstatically answered, "Yes."

We then went downstairs where a white stretch limousine was waiting for us. He wouldn't tell me our destination, but we eventually arrived at a lovely restaurant. We descended a staircase into a private room, which was filled with our friends and family—including Susan, who deserved an Oscar for her performance. The proposal and the surprise engagement party were absolutely magical.

—*Peggy Rose, Newport Coast, CA*

COME SAIL AWAY

Chris, my fiance, and I have had an ongoing competition throughout our three-year relationship. We have taken great pride in seeing who can surprise the other the most. He won with his proposal.

Chris races sailboats as a hobby, and sailing has always been something we enjoy doing together. There is one boat in particular that has been the setting of many milestones in our relationship. One day, Chris told me we were going out on the boat to raft up (tie up with a bunch of other boats) and spend the day celebrating a victory with his teammates.

When we had been afloat for about two hours, the sun became rather ruthless and I suggested we raise the sail for some shade because we were anchored. While his teammates raised the mainsail, Chris asked me to help him with something. As we finished, I turned around. Written on the sail was "Kate, will you marry me?"

I looked down, and there was Chris on his knee with a ring in his hand asking me to spend the rest of my life with him. I immediately said yes. He kissed me and then whispered in my ear, "I got you."

—*Kate Merton, Edgewater, MD*

TALE AS OLD AS TIME

*L*ast year for Christmas, my boyfriend flew me to New York City to see *Beauty and the Beast* and *The Lion King* on Broadway. It is very difficult to get tickets for these shows, but he had bought them back in October when we first met and started dating. We had not been dating for very long, so I was surprised that he had gotten me such an extravagant gift. He called it our "make-it-or-break-it" weekend. I guess we made it.

This summer, *Beauty and the Beast* came to our hometown of Boston. Once again, my boyfriend had planned ahead. On July 3, he told me to get dressed up because we were going to a very romantic restaurant for dinner and then to see a show. The restaurant was on top of the Prudential building and we had a window table. Dinner was delicious and the view was beautiful.

After dinner, we drove to the theater. Up until that point, he had been quite secretive as to which show we were going to see. When I discovered it was *Beauty and the Beast,* I was very touched. We even had front row seats this time. My boyfriend sat on the aisle and I sat next to him. After intermission, during which he drank a glass of beer in about one sip, we switched seats.

About fifteen minutes into the second half of the show, Belle came down the grand stairway in her golden gown to meet the Beast. Mrs. Potts started singing "Tale as old as time. . . ." At that moment, my boyfriend leaned in close to me and whispered, "I love you."

I answered, "Yeah, I love you, too. Now watch the show." Before I could get the last word out, he slipped a ring on my finger and asked, "Will you marry me?"

As excited as I'd been to see *Beauty and the Beast,* I never could have guessed that the romantic highlight of the show would take place in the audience! Of course, I said yes. I had no idea that he would be asking me any time soon. Apparently, he had been putting money away for a ring since our first big date in New York City. He even asked my parents for their permission. What a guy!

—*Jennifer Lehane, Marlborough, MA*

GARDEN OF EDEN

Mario Fulgieri and I began dating approximately five and a half years ago. Around our one-year anniversary, I left New York to attend graduate school in Connecticut. Prior to my departure, Mario carved our initials in a tree on the grounds of our alma mater as an expression of his love and commitment to me. It was a very memorable moment in our relationship.

After four years of graduate school and an internship in Pennsylvania, I returned to New York and the love of my life. Two weeks after my return, Mario suggested that we take a bicycle ride through the park near our college. We packed our bikes into the car and were on our way.

While driving, Mario suggested that we stop by "our tree" first. I thought nothing of this because we often visited it to gaze at our initials, which were still visible despite the time that had passed. I was excited to see our tree for the first time since my return to New York.

As I stepped out of the car and walked toward the tree, I noticed something unusual. The tree was adorned with beautiful potted plants and flowers. Bushes surrounded the tree, creating a little alcove—our own little Garden of Eden. On a patch of fresh sod was a small table, which was beautifully decorated with a lace tablecloth, a vase filled with pink carnations, two hand-painted glasses, a bottle of champagne, caviar, crackers, pastries, bread, and cheese. By the table were two small wicker chairs. A small radio played "The Way You Look Tonight" by Frank Sinatra.

Above our carved initials on the tree, Mario had hung three heart-shaped plaques that read "Marry Me, Melissa."

I couldn't believe Mario had gone to so much trouble. When I turned in amazement to face him, he was on bended knee, proclaiming his everlasting love for me and asking me to be his wife. How could I say no?

We rejoiced in our Eden for most of the afternoon. Many friends and family, as well as some strangers, dropped by to congratulate us on our new beginning.

—Melissa D. Elsner, Massapequa Park, NY

THIS LITTLE PIGGY

$\mathcal{I}$t was early in the morning on Mother's Day. As I woke up, I felt a tingling pain in my toe. I figured it was just one of the corns on my toe that was bothering me, so I paid it no mind. I tried to go back to sleep, but the pain started to get irritating. Finally, I reached down under the covers. Instead of a corn, I felt what appeared to be a ring on my toe. My eyes popped open and I was suddenly wide awake. I pulled the ring off my toe and took it out from under the covers. It was a diamond ring!

My boyfriend was nowhere to be found. A minute later, he walked into our bedroom and said, "Oh, you're awake." I was absolutely speechless. Then he said, "I see you found the ring. So, you think you want to spend the rest of your life with me and have my babies?" I happily said, "Of course," and we were married a few months later.

—*Stacey Johnson, Lithonia, GA*

A ROSE BY ANY OTHER NAME

*D*uring my spring break from graduate school, I visited my boyfriend at his school. The Thursday of that week marked our twenty-seventh month together, and he wanted us to have a date just like we used to when we were going to school together—buy each other dinner and a movie and go shopping at the mall. We planned to meet in the lobby of the dorm where I lived during my college years, because that was where he always picked me up for our dates.

When I arrived, my boyfriend was nowhere to be seen. On the desk in the lobby was a bundle of roses and a card. The envelope was addressed to me and labeled "Clue #1." There were four roses in the bundle. I opened the card and saw my boyfriend's handwriting:

> *This is the place in which we did learn*
> *Three days a week to think and discern.*
> *You know the seats in which we sat*
> *To sit and get cozy and take a nice hour's nap.*
> *Go there now, and you will find*
> *Your next clue to solve and unwind.*

I didn't have a clue what he was talking about. I finally realized that the clue was directing me to the chapel. At our college, we had chapel three times a week and we always sat together in the same seats. So off to the chapel I went. Across the seats where we used to sit were four more roses and an envelope marked "Clue #2." It read:

> *Clue number three could lead you to me*
> *All you can do is wait and see.*

Go to the place where you used to sit,
And bug kids for hours. You even got paid for it!

I was a student recruiter during my time at the college. I went to the office where I used to work. On the table were three more roses and another clue. At this point I was getting very suspicious about what was going on. I had told my boyfriend that I didn't want a dozen roses from anyone until they were ready to propose to me. I was now holding eleven roses. Clue #3 read:

Well, here you are, next to last stop.
You'll see me soon, so don't give up.
Go to the place we decided to date,
Twenty-seven months ago, and don't be late.

I ran back to my car and drove down to the lake where he first asked me to be his girlfriend. As I drove into the parking lot, I saw his car. As I got out of my car, he got out of his and I saw he was wearing his tuxedo. I also noticed that he was holding one rose in his hands. I started bawling. He had a big smile on his face.

"How many roses do you have?" he asked.

"Eleven," I replied, my voice shaking.

"So, I guess this makes twelve," he said, handing me the twelfth rose.

As I took it from him, I noticed a beautiful diamond ring tucked inside the petals. He got down on one knee and said, "All I want to do is make you happy for the rest of your life. Will you marry me?"

I don't even think I said yes. I think I just nodded and he slipped the ring on my finger.

—*Shilo Cowles, Warsaw, IN*

A BY-THE-BOOK PROPOSAL

*W*e are very honored that the writer of the following story has chosen our book to express her love for her boyfriend. She shares her feelings in the following heartfelt letter, which is sure to take Greg by surprise when he reads it for the first time in this book.

Dear Greg,

Do you believe in love at first sight? I do. I remember the first time I saw you at the bar, Kicker's. You were standing in front of the first booth by the stage as my brother and I approached. He introduced us to each other and that's where it all began. Our love for dancing bonded us, and the rest is history. You boot-scooted right into my heart.

We are two of a kind . . . inseparable indeed. You are my very best friend and the love of my life. I feel I'm the luckiest woman in the world when I get to spend time alone with you. My dream is that we can be together forever, and I hope you feel the same. Just knowing that we'll be stuck with each other will make us even happier than we are now. Could it be? No, I don't think that we could be any happier! I can't imagine life before you. You are everything to me. You never know when you're going to need love. (Bet you thought I'd say scissors, eh?)

We have been together for almost four years, and I wanted to tell you how much you mean to me by expressing it in this book. Everyone who reads this can see the love I have for you. Every day we're together feels like the very first day we met. You are the most perfect man and I want you all to myself. Besides, you're always willing to take me to the emergency room whenever I need to go! I wanted to beat you to it, and I thought it would be a fabulous surprise.

So, Greg Sousek: Will you marry me? Just say "Yes!"

Love, Laura

—Laura Schuman, Milwaukee, WI

If you or someone you know has a great proposal story that you would like to share with the authors, please forward it to:

Just Say Yes!
P.O. Box 36881
Los Angeles, CA 90036

Justsayyesbook@yahoo.com

ABOUT THE AUTHORS

Kathryn Mills is a publicist
for a publishing company. She
has a bachelor's degree in marketing from Ohio State University. She resides with her
husband, Bob, and her beagle,
Daisy, in Los Angeles.

PHOTO BY ROB MAY

Appel, Ginther & Mills

Debbie Appel is a freelance writer who has a bachelor's degree in
sociology from UCLA and a master's degree in writing and publishing
from Emerson College. She resides in Los Angeles.

Kristan Ginther is a freelance writer who has written for such publications as *Boxoffice* magazine, *LA Weekly,* and the *New York Resident.*
She has bachelor's degrees in journalism and communications from
the University of Wisconsin—Madison. She resides in Los Angeles
with her husband, Dan.